PENGUIN BOOKS

THE BEST THING ON TV

Director of the Shakespeare Institute, video artist, and critic, Jonathan Price is the author of *Life Show: How to See Theater in Life and Life in Theater* (with John Lahr) and *Video Visions,* a book about do-it-yourself TV and experimental video art. He has a doctorate in fine arts from Yale University but claims that educational TV puts him to sleep; commercials do more faster, he says—"they're the closest thing to video art on television." Price lives in New York City and likes Chocodiles, Pop Rocks, Lapsang Souchong tea, Puma sneakers, Lao-tse, Mao, Li Po, the Stones, meat loaf, Claes Oldenburg, dancing, and washing dishes. He makes great spaghetti and fudge and once painted all sixty-four *I Ching* hexagrams on five blocks of cobblestones on New York City's West Side Highway—"for strollers and bicyclers." He sometimes answers his mail.

the best thing on TV
COMMERCIALS
jonathan price

PENGUIN BOOKS

Penguin Books Ltd, Harmondsworth,
Middlesex, England
Penguin Books, 625 Madison Avenue,
New York, New York 10022, U.S.A.
Penguin Books Australia Ltd, Ringwood,
Victoria, Australia
Penguin Books Canada Limited, 2801 John Street,
Markham, Ontario, Canada L3R 1B4
Penguin Books (N.Z.) Ltd, 182–190 Wairau Road,
Auckland 10, New Zealand

First published in the United States of America and Canada in
simultaneous hardcover and paperback editions by
The Viking Press and Penguin Books 1978

LIBRARY OF CONGRESS CATALOGING IN PUBLICATION DATA
Price, Jonathan, 1941–
The best thing on TV: commercials.
1. Television advertising. I. Title.
HF6146.T42P74   659.14'3   78-17717
ISBN 0 14 00.5004 3

Printed in the United States of America by
Kingsport Press, Inc., Kingsport, Tennessee
Set in Linotype Baskerville and CRT Helvetica Light

PHOTO ACKNOWLEDGMENTS

I gratefully acknowledge permission to reproduce photographs from: Abbott Laboratories, Inc.; After Six, Inc.; Alfa Romeo, Inc.; Allegheny Airlines; American Airlines; American Express Co.; American Motors Corp.; American Tourister; Ames, Inc.; Arm & Hammer Division, Church & Dwight Co., Inc.; Dick de Bartolo; Bassett Furniture Industries, Inc.; Bic Pen Corp.; Black & Decker Mfg. Co.; Blue Cross/Blue Shield of Greater New York; Borden, Inc.; Buick Motor Division, General Motors Corp.; Leo Burnett USA; Cadbury Corp.; Chevrolet Motor Division, General Motors Corp.; Chrysler Motor Corp.; Compton Advertising, Inc.; The Conair Corp.; The Continental Insurance Companies; Coty Division of Pfizer, Inc.; Dannon Milk Products, Division of Beatrice Foods Co.; Dolphin Productions; E. C. Publications, Inc.; Emery Air Freight Corp.; Excello Corp.; Ferrero USA, Inc.; Fiat, Inc.; General Motors Corp.; Genesee Brewing Co., Inc.; Gillette Co.; Green Giant Co.; GTE Sylvania, Inc.; Hallmark Cards, Inc.; Hamm's Beer; The Hartford Insurance Group; Hershey Foods Corp.; ITT Corp.; Jones Dairy Farms, Inc.; Kraft, Inc.; Lever Brothers Co.; Louis Marx & Co.; Master Lock Co.; Matchbox; MEM Co., Inc.; Midas; Miles Laboratories, Inc.; Miller-Morton Co.; MONY—Mutual of New York; National Airlines, Inc.; National Car Rental System, Inc.; PepsiCo, Inc.; Peter Paul, Inc.; Pontiac Motor Division, General Motors Corp.; Qantas Airways Ltd.; Reynolds Metals Co.; Ronzoni Macaroni Co., Inc.; Royal Crown Cola Co.; Sabena Belgian World Airlines; Scholl, Inc.; Southwestern Bell; Stevens Hosiery, Inc.; Stouffer's, Inc.; Thermos Division, King-Seeley Thomas Co.; Timex Corp.; Angelo Torres; Union Underwear Co., Inc.; United Press International; Volkswagen of America, Inc.; Volvo of America, Inc.; Waring Products Division, Dynamics Corp. of America; Warner Books, Inc.; Welch Foods, Inc.; West Bend Co.; Weyerhaeuser Co.; Wolf Brand Products, subsidiary of Quaker Oats Co.; Xerox Corp.

contents

acknowledgments

first, a hosannah for Sandy Haver, a Pontiac cheer for George Lois, a noisy meow for Jerry Della Femina, wild applause for such magnificent storytellers as Barry Biederman, Joe Brown, Ed Buxton, Howard Cohen, Irv Drasnin, Amil Gargano, Norman Geller, Milt Gossett, Mel Helitzer, Ron Hoff, Jack Keil, Alex Kroll, Joe Lamneck, Marce Mayhew, Albert and David Maysles, Charlie Moss, Bryan Olesky, Stafford Ordahl, John O'Toole, Don Sibray, Alan Stanley, and Bob Warner. A trumpet fanfare for Susan Farrell, Joan Graham, Karen Gregory, Harold Gully, Barbara Hunzinger Harnett, Joyce Harrington, Susan Irwin, Jenny Marjollet, Patty McManus, Toni Meyer, Barbara Oka, and Marilyn Woloz. Another Clio for Bill Evans, a platinum CB radio for Bill Fries, and a Hallelujah chorus for Amanda Vaill and Elizabeth McKee.

And a happy wave of thanks to Jerome Ahlbrand, Edson Allen, Gordon Alloway, Carl Ally, Alan Anderson, Armand Arel, Marshall Barrett, Sheldon Bart, Marty Benson, James Bernardin, Jack Bernstein, Don Bittner, James Blocki, Ken Boys, Caroline Bracie, Howard Brod, Ned Brown, William Brown, Jr., Robert Buchanan, Russell Burnham, Don Carlos, Thomas Charbonneau, Lexie Chasman, Sue Chiafullo, Mel Clapman, Sylvester Cleary, Al Coleman, Joseph Cooper, Ron Corser, Ralph Countryman, Gwyn Cravens, Wilson Crook, Jr., Susan Danehower, Hal Davis, Craig Denton, Ranjana Dikhit, J. T. Doyle, James Edris, Kristin Elliott, William Elliott, Tom Engelman, Joseph Falsetti, Frank Filtsch, Murray Firestone, James Flynn, Jack Francis, Web Francis, Barry Fulford, D. M. Furman, F. Joseph Gallagher, Jr., Caleb Gattegno, Allyn Glaub, Lawrence Glucs, Paul Gold, Sterling Green, Louise Heikes, Tony Hiss, J. P. Hogan, Stephanie Hunt, Stuart Hunt, J. Thomas Hurley, Murray Hysen, Michael Isser, William Jackson, Bruce Johnson, David Johnson, William Johnson, Russell Kahn, Burton Kehoe, Ed Kelly, J. L. Kennedy, William Killen, Ben Kimbrough, Sol Koffler, Richard Kotz, T. E. Latimer, Robert Leonard, Robert Lepre, Jeff Lewis, John Lippman, John Litchfield, John Lowden, David Lubeck, F. Bradley Lynch, William Lyon, William MacFarland, Jack Maged, Pat Mahoney, Joe Markowski, Dick Martin, John Mason, Alan Mayer, G. W. Mentch, R. T. Miller, Max Mittelman, Michael Mohamad, Lanning Molnar, Rosemarie Montagna, Douglas Morgan, Sally Nagy, The Network Project, Richard Nickson, Larry Nunno, J. A. Oaks, Dean Oberpriller, Carroll O'Rourke, Giorgio Pavia, Larry Plapler, Ingrid Rauch, Richard Rosenbloom, Ron Rosenfeld, Nancy Ryan, Thomas Ryan, Ron Salvo, Hal Savage, Sam Scali, Robert Schmidt, Richard Schoonover, Lester Schwartz, Jill Seligson, Gerald Shapiro, H. K. Shaw, Robert Siemers, Gail Smith, Patti Smith, Nadine Sprangers, Burt Staniar, Marty Stern, Philip Stevens, Mark Stroock, Joseph Sullivan, Joseph Sullivano, Robert Sundmacher, Milton Sutton, Norman Sylvester, Angela Tedesco, Jack Temares, Mike Temares, W. S. Thomas, M. C. Tobias, Bernard Toll, Jim Tower, Lou Tripodi, Paul Truntlich, Alice Uniman, Richard Wiebe, Edward Wilson, James Winton, Dale Worcester.

More fun than a gorilla with a suitcase, more explosive than a camera that blows up, more entertaining than the programs they interrupt, more informative than most network news, commercials are often the best thing on TV. And the best commercials outpace the television programs they sponsor in at least a dozen ways.

■ Commercials are dangerous to make: The admen who go out on location often risk their lives for even less than an Oscar; they do death-defying stunts for the sake of five seconds of film to advertise a car—or peanut butter.

■ They're violent to products: Unlike regular programs, commercials don't hurt people; they torture products.

■ They're almost obscene: Also unlike regular programs, commercials hint and flash but never deliver; the suggestions are enough to arouse, but these clean scenes never come to climax.

■ They're emotional: In thirty seconds, not thirty minutes, a commercial can make your eyes moisten, your adrenaline accelerate, and your heart thump.

■ They're coldly calculated: Since a commercial is designed as part of a marketing strategy, its objectives are studiously worked out beforehand; compared to program writers, the creators of commercials are far more conscious of the impact they are making.

■ They're carefully written: Since every second costs more than two thousand dollars, crack writers sand every idea and plan every camera angle for maximum effect, making the authors of *60 Minutes* look like tourists casually writing home.

■ They're overdirected: Shooting one hundred feet of film for every one they use, commercial directors caress every detail until it glows: particularly on food, hair, and cars, the results are bravura.

■ They're star-studded: There are more Oscar winners playing the breaks than the shows, and commercials sometimes turn unknowns into superstars in a few months.

■ They're extravagantly produced: Since more money goes into the production of some thirty-second spots than into half-hour shows, commercials often have flashier locations, bigger casts, stranger sets, snappier graphics, and funnier ideas.

■ They're highly edited: Our culture is learning faster perception per second thanks to editing techniques that show us a hundred bottles of beer on a wall in twenty-seven seconds, or sixty-five pictures of McDonald's breakfasts in sixty seconds; we follow them, and when we return to the slower editing of regular programming—not to mention the scenes of real life—we may find the pace unaccountably dull.

■ They're regulated and censored: Commercials have to submit to many more censors and many more taboos than regular programming; since freedom of expression does not apply to advertisers, the commercials must do a fine tap dance down the line of conventions, a discipline that keeps commercials politically agile and diplomatically astute.

■ They're even rated PG: When parents cannot ban products, they band together to prevent advertisers from mentioning the rotten stuff to kids; as a result, ads to children are now much more honest than the programs—and kids still like candy.

Culturally, commercials have trained our eye to accept fast cuts, dense and highly paced imagery, very brief scenes, connections that are implied but not spelled out—in brief, a new style of visual entertainment.

Historically, we see commercials more often than the shows (the same spot may be run six to sixty times a season), and we recall them in more detail, often with more fondness. People feel great nostalgia for the White Knight, the Green Giant, Speedy Alka-Seltzer, Tony the Tiger, Snap, Crackle, and Pop—these are the elves of our country's imagination.

Financially, commercials represent the pinnacle of our popular culture's artistic expression. More money per second goes into their making, more cash flows from their impact, more business thinking goes into each word than in any movie, opera, stage play, painting, or videotape. If commercials are artful, then the art is objective, not subjective; capitalist, not rebellious; part of a social activity rather than a personal search for expression; more like a Roman road than a lyric poem. Their beauty is economic.

CLASSICS

AJAX CLEANSER
White Knight   1963

ALKA-SELTZER
Speedy   1953

BUFFERIN
A's and B's   1952

CREST TOOTHPASTE
Look, Mom, No Cavities   1958

HERTZ RENT A CAR
Puts You in the Driver's Seat   1961

MARLBORO CIGARETTES
The Marlboro Man   1955

MISS CLAIROL
Does She or Doesn't She?   1957

MURIEL CIGARS
Come Up and Smoke Me   1951

OLD GOLD CIGARETTES
Dancing Packs   1950

PEPSODENT TOOTHPASTE
Wonder Where the Yellow Went   1956

ZEST SOAP
Feel Really Clean   1960

Remember these golden oldies? They all won the designation "classic" from the people who hand out the annual Oscars of the commercial world, the Clios.

Yes, some are dumb. Some guy leaning out of the screen to yell at us because we supposedly tried to make him change beers just makes us hate Schlitz. People going gaga when they walk into a bank, just because the bank accepts savings accounts, make me gag. But then I don't love Lucy much. And I'm glad Gilligan has to stay on his island.

Commercials are not all superb. But the best are lively, very American mini-dramas, tiny films, high-speed epics. Taken as a whole, commercials offer a rough catalogue of our consumer economy and a wild tour of our unconscious fantasies.

In 1948, when TV first started to reach a large audience, commercials went over the air live. For twenty years radio had fed on commercials, and now that the radio networks were branching out into TV, they borrowed the technique of reading copy at the moment they were broadcasting —live. But it wasn't as simple as that—the cameras presented new problems. Announcers got stage fright and had to be pushed into the lighted areas. "The mistakes and mishaps were nightmarish for advertisers," says Ed Buxton, author of *Promise Them Anything*. "The dog that refused to eat the pet food...the announcer who praised the wrong brand name... the electrician who walked across in front of the camera...the actress whose breast fell out of her low-cut gown."

Fed up, ad agencies turned to film in the mid-Fifties. Some set up studios in their own offices, but the resultant confusion grew intolerable, so most agencies hired companies that had been making industrial films to make commercials for them. Often they used recognizable stars: Bing Crosby opened his Philco refrigerator, took out a can of Minute Maid orange juice, and then just talked about it. Red Skelton polished his car on camera with Instant J-Wax, talking as he rubbed. Despite the use of live actors, many scripts still sounded like a print ad being read aloud. But gradually, the stand-up announcer

GREEN GIANT Spanning 26 years, the Green Giant starts out rough, then gets streamlined and spawns a young sprout.

holding a product gave way to location shots, dramas, musicals. Jars and cans began to talk. Bufferin cut away the skin and showed how headaches pound and stomachs bubble. Speedy Alka-Seltzer, the animated tablet, made his appearance—although he did little more than talk at the camera. Cigarette packs danced and clapped. "Critics acclaimed these spots as 'better than the programs' on television at the time," Buxton recalls. "By the mid-Sixties they were not only *tours de force* of entertainment, but enormously expensive." Betty Crocker was going to Europe to demonstrate a new recipe; movie stars added glamour and expense to hair-spray spots; admen began devising stunts so complicated they had to call on NASA for help. These top-dollar budgets drew some first-rate still photographers into the business, and at the same time, art directors and writers started looking at commercials as potentially "great films."

The late Sixties became the golden age of arty commercials. Until then most admen had focused on print; TV had gotten much less attention. For five or six years, though, beginning in 1964, admen experimented with TV, learning how to use the camera, how to work within a sixty-second limit, how to tell short stories, how to make mini-films; during this period most admen finally learned how to make commercials themselves. When Dick Rich and Stewart Greene took over the Alka-Seltzer account in 1964, for example, they killed off the mind-melting mascot, Speedy Alka-Seltzer, as too cute, too old. Rich came up with the new slogan, "No matter what shape your stomach's in," and Greene arranged for brief films of twenty-three tummies bouncing, bubbling, being beaten. Sascha Berlin wrote the tune. Sales started up, and the song became a gold platter (one million copies of the jingle sold). Ron Rosenfeld axed Miss Rheingold and replaced her with the ethnic pitch: "In New York, where there are more (fill in: Jews, Italians, Irish, Greeks) than in all of (Jerusalem, Venice,

ANNOUNCER: Never insert cotton swab tips into ear canal to remove wax.

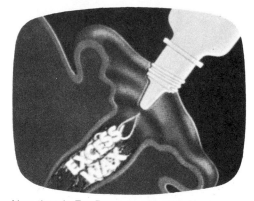

Now there's Ear Drops and Ear Washer by Murine. Murine's Ear Drops gently, safely soften hard excess wax when used as directed.

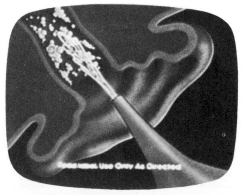

Then Murine's Ear Washer gently washes wax away so pressure and pain are relieved.

Dublin, Sparta), more people drink Rheingold than any other beer." Sex came on strong: "Turn me loose, let me laugh and make love—Imprévu." Initial reaction from viewers was rave. "My television set was dormant for five years," one woman told *Newsweek* at the time (1966). "Those commercials are so good that I look forward to them. It's the programs that drive me away." Commented *Newsweek*: "The brassy hard sell still exists, but more and more products are turning to the soft sell, the sexy sell, or the star sell. And not only are the commercials better than the programs they sponsor, they often cost more."

But not everyone bought more. In 1967 *The New Yorker*'s Talk of the Town writers reported a party at which everyone was reciting a favorite commercial. "A few more questions established the fact that none of the admirers of the Rheingold campaign had ever been tempted to try the product, and when we pursued the matter further, it turned out that no one in the entire group could remember increasing his daily consumption of Alka-Seltzer or Ajax.... The job of the TV commercial, of course, is to turn viewers into consumers, but it seems that when the TV commercial is at its best, certain people in the audience become consumers not of the products advertised but of the advertisements themselves." Sure enough, Alka-Seltzer sales leveled off; Rheingold drinkers turned out to be pleased to see their own ethnic groups, but not so happy to realize that "those other people" also drank it. When recession set in and sales dropped, the sponsors, who had paid for this wonderful learning experience for the admen, began to get angry over every penny they misspent.

1970 marks the turning point. Agencies tightened up and started testing commercials before they went on the air and just after; the copy-

---

MURINE In an old-fashioned diagram, we cut open an ear to see excess wax.

AD SPEAK

When you first meet the people who make commercials, you find they speak their own jargon. Here's a sampling of ad talk, with translations.

ACCUMULATED AUDIENCE This measurement of audience answers the sponsor's question: how many people saw our spot, at least once, in a given month?

ACCOUNT PEOPLE The liaison between ad agency and the sponsor, selling the agency's ideas to the client, and bringing back suggestions and complaints to the art director at the agency, for revisions.

AUDIENCE RECALL Various testing services find out how much an audience actually remembers after seeing a commercial. On average, a quarter of the audience will recall the basic message.

COST PER THOUSAND Sponsors pay the television station for the privilege of reaching a certain number of people, of a given age and sex; the cost per thousand people varies enormously, though, from local news shows to the Superbowl.

CREATIVE DIRECTOR OF THE WORLD A normal creative director supervises the work of teams of writers and artists within one agency; when he gets promoted, he bosses the creative directors in every branch around the world. Hence, this megalomaniac title.

CREATIVE SIDE The writers, artists, and technicians who actually make the commercials. ("He's in creative.")

DOWNSCALE Poor people in the audience for a given TV show.

FLIGHTING Running commercials in short bursts, a week on, a week off, for instance; scheduling spots in an in-and-out pattern.

FREQUENCY Average number of times a viewer gets exposed to a spot.

GROSS IMPRESSIONS Total number of times people may have received some impression from a commercial, answering the sponsor's question: how many people saw an ad how many times, all told? Another word for it: Tonnage.

HUT Homes using television, as measured by the Nielsen Company.

MEDIA BUYER A savvy negotiator, a specialist who decides which TV program, on what day, would draw the most people who might buy the product being advertised.

REACH Total number of people or homes reached at least once by a commercial.

SHOOT The actual "shooting" of film or video-tape to be used in the commercial.

STORYBOARD The script for a commercial, with dialogue and drawings of the scenes.

WRAP Last phase in making a commercial, in which the editor, art director, account executive, and sponsor wrap up the final version.

writers and art directors who had played around during the Sixties became responsible executives and closed the doors on any younger people who might want to learn the trade by making some expensive boo-boos; the watchword became "Back to Basics," and everyone announced that they favored no-nonsense, straightforward, product-oriented brand-name ads plugging a single major benefit. "The hippie fashionable advertising of the past wasted a tremendous amount of money," said adman John Bowen later; his advertising agency, Benton & Bowles, now uses the slogan, "It's not creative unless it sells." So we're back to the Bayer blindfold test and singing cats and construction workers saying, "How do you spell relief? I spell it Rolaids."

Early in 1976 *Newsweek* had to admit that things had changed. "The trend today has evolved toward an older, simpler style, with commercials taking their cue from the vindictive chant of 'Ring around the collar' or the Charmin grocer, George Whipple, furtively squeezing a roll of toilet paper. 'The buzz word today is hard sell,' says adman Jerry Della Femina. 'You may hate those ads, and I may hate those ads, but the point is they work. They sell.' "

But the biggest event in the recent history of commercials was not the return of hard-sell spots —they had never really gone away. The major change was a shift of length: from one minute, commercials shrank to thirty seconds. Costs had gone up, and tests showed that a thirty-second commercial could make almost two-thirds the impact of a sixty, so the smart money went to the shorter time. Many writers felt stranded, baffled. How could they fit enough into forty-five words? How could they make a sale with only twenty-eight and a half seconds of audio? Now there was no time for mood, for leisurely movies imitating *Zorba the Greek* or *Woman in the Dunes* such as Rosenfeld had done for his Greek and Japanese spots for Rheingold.

For the first time, commercials could no longer ape the movies. They had to act as fast as regular TV. Most programs on TV are really like short movies: they indulge in what movies do well—lots of long shots with beautiful scenery, nice slow scenes dwelling on people in conflict, realistic pictures; if someone goes out the door, he has to go down the steps before we see him entering the car. But TV can work much faster by using a kind of ellipsis, and over the last seven years commercials have trained us to grasp what gets left out when we see someone open his front door, then—in a quick cut—get into his car. Many more shots got crammed into such a short space, too. Fast cuts became faster. No one could waste the half-second extra time to dissolve from one scene to the next: you had to snap, shock, and jolt. During the early Seventies the men and women who had learned how to make beautiful short movies back in the Sixties finally started making real TV.

Within thirty seconds we may now find three brief scenes in which people use the product, a quick flash of the product itself, plus one more vignette at the end. The structure resembles that of *The Waltons* or *Little House on the Prairie*: a few problems, a big well-lit moment with Mom and Dad working out "the solution," then the payoff, in which the solution works. But the commercial, mercifully, is briefer.

Some sponsors are even moving into the ten-second length. Publishers find they can afford to sell books like detergent, at the lower cost per second; surely ten seconds is enough to communicate the gist of a book. Why, for this book, I can imagine flashing fifteen frames from favor-ite commercial spots from 1948 to the present while the announcer says, "The Best Thing on TV . . . You saw it first on television . . . Now it's a great book from Viking Penguin." Then for the last three seconds we see a copy of the book.

Why not? Tests prove viewers cannot remember commercials that say two things or more, so most spots develop one USP (unique selling proposition) and focus on that. If you only have one thing to say, you should be able to say it in ten seconds. Nowadays when a copywriter gets a chance to write a commercial that is sixty or ninety seconds long, for a special, say, he imagines the Kansas prairie stretching out in front of him forever. It's an epic.

Of course, in the old days in the nine and a half minutes allocated to commercials you got only nine spots because each lasted a minute, with the extra time given to the station to plug its other shows. Now you get at least nineteen spots in the same time—more if the station indulges in ten-second spots—and even faster ads for up-coming shows. This mess is called clutter. Because a viewer faces so many different appeals in each break, the programs seem like sand dunes of calm—relaxing, not too demanding, perhaps a bit boring. In most shows, if you miss ten minutes you can pick up the plot thread in a few lines of dialogue. In a commercial, if you

SPEEDY: Plop, plop, fizz, fizz, oh, what a relief it is . . .

ALKA-SELTZER Mascot, puppy, and cherub, Speedy has not vanished from memory, though flash-ier commercial ideas wiped him off the air during the creative boom of the mid-Sixties.

turn around you've missed the whole thing. So copywriters feel even more pressure to grab you, shock you, surprise you.

Money increases this pressure, too, since the cost per second keeps rising. Back when Milton Berle hosted the *Texaco Star Theater* in the early Fifties, the average weekly production budget for the whole show ran $15,000. Now you could hardly produce one thirty-second commercial for that, much less get it on the air. An average commercial now can cost from $20,000 to $60,000, and a lot more for special effects. In the mid-Sixties one minute on prime time on a network would cost you around $30,000; by the mid-Seventies the cost had just about doubled ($50,000–$60,000), but time on major specials and blockbuster movies had jumped to $200,000 a minute. (That's over $3,000 a second.) During 1976 the top 554 advertisers spent over $3 billion on TV ads, about half of the total. The leaders spent as follows:

Procter & Gamble:	$193 million
General Foods:	$128 million
Bristol-Myers:	$102 million
American Home:	$97 million
General Motors:	$72 million

By 1977 the World Series was selling at $75,000 for every thirty seconds. Gillette, Chevrolet, Miller Brewing, and Firestone Tire & Rubber each spent more than $1 million for such brief spots. And Super Bowl XII was going at $325,000 a minute.

Joe Ostrow, who "buys time" for Young & Rubicam's clients—he selects the programs, chooses the slots, and pays for his clients' TV advertising—accused the networks of operating like a cartel in "their lust for greater and greater profitability." And Herbert Maneloveg, a major expert on the costs of advertising in different media (magazines, TV, radio), called on advertisers to band together to demand a halt to the TV price hikes. But most media-buyers pooh-poohed these charges and smiled. During 1977, in fact, advertisers devoted almost 55 percent of their budget to network and spot TV, compared to magazines (20 percent), newspapers (15.7 percent), radio (6.4 percent) and billboards (2.6 percent).

Why this continued devotion to TV in the face of rising—even outrageous—prices? TV commercials *do* sell—not all of them, not all the time, but often enough so business can time the upsurge of sales from the minute their spot aired on *The Doctors.* Back in 1950 Hazel Bishop put its whole ad budget into TV; before TV the cosmetics firm grossed $50,000 a year in sales; with two years of TV spots, their sales topped $4,500,000. For new products, TV can create a national market within a month; for standard brands like Colgate, twelve spots a week, minimum, keep people buying. The consensus among American marketing managers is that if you sell to individuals across the country—if you retail to the mass audience—you must use TV for major impact. The only important industries that ignore TV sell to executives, not consumers —printers, hospital suppliers, manufacturers of industrial chemicals and ventilation equipment.

With all this money being spent and earned, with styles changing every few years, with each second carrying a huge price tag, commercials reflect the rough pace, the competitive tension, and the calculator imagination of American capitalism. These electronic vignettes—part real, part fantasy—are charged with the greed, the fear, the lust, the patriotic self-deceptions, even the fellow-feeling of all Americans. And precisely because underneath the glossy surface of what we see at home on TV lie the imaginings of a creative person, and because these ideas so often take root in our own unconscious, growing later into action, purchase, and attitude, commercials can be dangerous. Certainly they can be downright dangerous to make. But that is part of what makes commercials the best thing on TV.

Making commercials can be more dangerous than *Emergency*. At home we may feel so safe that no matter what accident occurs in a commercial, we may imagine that it is "not real." But in the frantic effort to get us to pay attention and not to forget, ad writers sometimes come up with scripts that get their actors, their whole crew into trouble so real it hurts. Under the client's pressure to score high in the audience's recall, ad writers nervously talk in terms borrowed from battle: they aim to set off a depth charge in the audience's mind, they plan to blast us with their message, to stun, to jolt, to strafe us.

Usually the wounds are superficial. But not if you are a condor: "Somebody was shooting an airline commercial, and they were going to use a condor to simulate flight," says Bryan Olesky, associate creative director at the ad agency Bozell & Jacobs. "Everyone was ready—they were below a plateau where they were going to let the bird go, and the director gave the signal, and they yelled, 'Release the condor!' Well, they threw the bird up, and somehow they had gotten a bird that didn't fly. Film crews from New York don't know much about birds. These guys couldn't have told a condor from a Mercury Montego. So this bird went up in the air and plummeted about two hundred feet straight down. The crew was filming, and the actors were acting, and the bird went straight down and splattered. And from then on, 'Release the condor' has been a standing joke in the business."

Although the condor was past appreciating the fact, most risks in the TV ad business are calculated. The writer figures the commercial has got to make your heart jump in order to prove that his paper can hold up under stress or that his bags are waterproof. To show how tough polyethylene film can be when St. Regis makes it, Stafford Ordahl, a top creative man at Cunningham & Walsh, took a movie crew to a small village in Spain. "We stretched two layers of quite thin plastic film across the street and had a fighting bull run into it. He could get his horn through it, but he couldn't get any farther. The people in that town were betting on the bull."

Ordahl made up a bridge out of St. Regis cardboard to show it could support a two-ton car over an announcer's head. No one knew whether the Mercedes would crush the announcer. But St. Regis paper wanted a dramatic demonstration of the superior technology in their cardboard boxes. "So we built this bridge out of ordinary cardboard, standard triple wall, thirteen feet high, about a hundred feet long, nothing but paper. We hired an architect to design the bridge. We shot this commercial in an airplane hangar in Burbank, California, because we needed a big area. We couldn't do it outside, because if it rained, it would have been all over. It was very expensive to build; it took us two weeks to make the paper bridge. And they were supposed to build it right under the center line in the roof. But for some reason they built it just to the side. We had a stunt driver. The driver, as he went up one side, was looking straight up at the ceiling. He couldn't see the bridge, so he was using the roof center-line as a guide. Inevitably, he edged to the right. He came within three inches of going over. Even after we explained to him, even after we put a guy in the rafters with a walkie-talkie, he still edged to the right. He missed going over the edge by a finger." But the bridge held up.

Barry Biederman, senior vice-president at Needham, Harper & Steers, decided to show off the no-skid brakes made by Teves, a German subsidiary of International Telephone and Telegraph, by photographing two cars coming toward him on a rain-slick highway. They jam on their brakes, and the one with no-skid stops safely, but the other one careens off the roadway. But instead of running into a tree, which might have been prohibitively dangerous, that

car would hit thin yellow sticks along the edge
of the road to suggest what *could* happen. The
cameraman would stand more or less in its path
to get all the action on film. "We worked this
all out very carefully, of course, with a jealous
regard for safety. There would be two cars
following each other very closely at sixty miles
an hour between these two rows of yellow sticks.
And at a certain point, each person would put
his brakes on. Well, at the first pass, the cars
didn't come close enough to the camera. We
wanted the same thing right up in front of it, so
we explained to our German drivers, you will
bring your car down closer to the camera. And
the two German drivers nodded and went back

while we got ourselves set up. Then the two
drivers decided between themselves that they
would go faster, which threw the whole calculation off. The second car ended up right where
we had been standing, so close to Ernie, our
cameraman, you could see the hair stand up on
his head. Ernie, being a professional, kept right
at his camera, and when it was over he got up,
and he sort of rocked back on his heels. He came
that close to being murdered. We would have
been wiped out."

Biederman specializes in high-risk commercials. Another subsidiary of ITT makes an under-
water pump that has worked for more than twelve
years submerged in the water that is sprayed

wall mining is a new technique here in the United States; in Europe they have used it for thirty years. In conventional mining, jackhammers punch away at the wall. But in long-wall mining, a grinder as tall as the wall moves along shearing off whole hunks of wall; these fall on a six-foot-wide conveyor belt that carries them thirty feet to a machine that grinds them up into three-inch bits, then dumps them on a hopper, to be hauled out by rail. This method can yield up to a hundred tons a day compared to forty tons the regular way. "We wanted people to see it's not a guy with a pickax. This is the new mining, *roarrrrr*.

"They took us down into a shaft. We each had a hardhat and a light. I was worried about poison gas. I kept looking for canaries to keel over, stuff like that. And you go down and down and down, and the elevator cage scrapes along the wall going down, and you're sure this is the day that elevator wire's going to give. Straight down sixteen hundred feet. Then we get in one of those cars, and they take us way back into the mine. When we get there, you've got to cross the conveyor belt. This belt has steel jaws that grab the coal and haul it down the tunnel to the pulverizer. It is called a pulverizer because it pulverizes things. And we get to this damn belt, and our guide, the foreman, steps over it. The trough has got to be about six feet across. Metal sides covered with a slick of coal dust and water. It couldn't be slipperier. And I'm wearing rubber boots that are covered with gook. And the foreman goes over, and he looks back, and the belt is going, and the guys in the mine are all looking at us. You got to cross, right? And I'm waiting for him to turn it off. But it doesn't stop, it just keeps going—*brrp, brrp, brr-rip*. I realized if I didn't go over, we'd never shoot the commercial.

"So I went over. To my great surprise I didn't slip onto the belt and land in the pulverizer. Then I looked back. Each guy, same thing. I

on a coal grinder to keep the dust down. Explosive conditions. In 1950 the ad writer would have drawn a diagram in the studio. But a diagram would not do; you had to see what foul murk that pump was functioning under. So, even though the mines might be a scary mess, even though explosions and cave-ins—not to mention claustrophobia—were a not-too-distant possibility, Biederman chose to shoot the commercial in a long-wall mine in Utah. Long-

MINOLTA Next spectacular: picture-taking in midair. They only lost one camera this way.

watched my buddies from the agency come up, look around, come over.

"So then we needed light. They had a four-thousand - one - hundred - and - sixty - volt power source for that machine. We had to bring in a transformer from Hollywood. It took six guys to move the damn thing through the tunnels to step the current down to one hundred and ten. Unbelievable. We didn't want to lose the darkness, so we strung lights at strategic points. But one of the problems is, the tunnel wall is still wet. And we were convinced we would have a mass electrocution."

They didn't, but the sponsor did get a scary commercial. We start out up on the surface, following a truck across the hot Utah desert. The announcer points out how dry the land is. We go into the mine, and suddenly it's dark and very wet. We hear water. We see slithery puddles. The foreman pulls a pump up from under the muck. It's working, he says. The place seems suffocating, noisy, claustrophobic. Biederman proves the pump is amazing—it's been functioning twenty-four hours a day for twelve years under this black mud. We fly away from the mine at the end, and we see tanks of water for irrigation. We can breathe again.

The decision to take some risks for the sake of drama starts off seeming logical—for the product, for its image, for the message—but the results are not so easy to calculate. Hamm's Beer, marketed from Chicago to the West Coast, had been running cartoon ads in the 1950's featuring a little cartoon bear; their slogan was, "From the land of sky-blue waters comes the beer refreshing." A writer who works at the ad agency Dancer-Fitzgerald-Sample says, "The image they had built over time was that of a big, outdoorsy beer, the pure beer from the sparkling clear water, and the guy who drank it pictured himself as a rugged man of the land, the woodsman, the logger. He may well have been a fat accountant living in Minneapolis, but the image

HAMM'S BEER Sasha, the bear, dips his paw in the water as his trainer navigates a lake near Hayfork, California.

he had of himself was this. Then in the mid-Sixties there was a management change, and when new management came in, they selected a new advertising agency, which came up with a new campaign. They said the cartoon bear was old-fashioned, and they tried a number of campaigns. And the mistake that agency made was that they didn't draw on the heritage of the beer. They tried to change it completely. And if you think about products you're familiar with, they all have an image. Oxydol—the image is the hard-working detergent for farmers, blue-collar workers; you'd never make that a sophisticated big-city kind of product. Volkswagen could never be sold as a luxury car; it's a practical, hard-working car. You could make a smaller Cadillac, you could make a very efficient car, and you could not sell it as a money-saver because the image is a luxury car. So the new campaign had nothing to do with the traditional image of Hamm's. There was one campaign called "A beer is a beer until you've had a Hamm's"—everyone around a bar, singing and horsing around. Well, you can sing a beer is a beer is a beer until you've had a Schlitz. You can put any name in there. And in advertising, if you can put any name in there, not just your product and your product alone, you may have trouble.

"And their sales continued down, so we went and did some research. We asked people what they thought of Hamm's and their advertising. This was in 1970–71. And do you know, they said, 'Oh yeah, Hamm's, that's the little cartoon bear, and from the land of sky-blue waters'? Now that advertising hadn't been on the air for five years. And that was what was coming back strong. The answer would seem to be, well, bring back the cartoon bear. But that wasn't so easy, because that was not really in tune with the times—it was a little hokey. It was old-fashioned. We wanted to create that same image, but do something different—bring it up-to-date. So we wrote a big song positioning it as a premium beer against Bud and Schlitz. We then created a man who'd be a little larger than life, walking, always walking through the woods, and he would stop off somewhere in a bar and have a beer, and then he'd start walking again. He'd walk away. And then on top of this we said, OK, bring back the bear.

"So we got a Kodiak bear, untrained, and we conditioned him, not trained him. This wasn't a dancing bear or a roller-skating bear. He still has all his claws on. But we spent six weeks. The man we chose is actually the bear's trainer. We had him grow a beard."

They found a little lumber town twelve miles beyond Hayfork, California. One gas station, four houses, a general store, and a bar. They sent in the film crews and director and actors and trailers and campers. Then the writer arrived, to discover there was no bear. "The director said, 'We got a problem.' And I said, 'I'll say we got a problem, if you don't know where the bear is. We got a bigger problem than you think!'"

The problem: no airline would fly the bear from New Jersey to San Francisco. Finally United agreed. "We got a call from the San Francisco airport: 'The man and the bear are now in an Econoline van, and they're driving up, and they should get there about nine o'clock at night.' Nine o'clock and we're all waiting—nothing; ten o'clock—nothing; one o'clock in the morning we hear the van. The door opens, and out gets the man. 'Yea, you're here!' we yell. 'Oh God, God, oh God,' he says and falls down. And we rush out to meet him to find out what's wrong. We got within twenty feet, and then we all started saying 'Oh God.' The bear had been carsick for one hundred and forty miles. He had vomited and defecated all over the inside of the van, all over both the driver and the assistant, and they just had to hang in there and drive. We got the doors open, and the bear is lying there with his feet up in the air. Ohhhhhh. It knocked a day out of our shooting,

the bear lying there moaning.

"Then, that first shot, when he comes over the hill and then down, and we're standing around the camera, and we're ready to shoot, and the man says, 'OK, the bear is loose,' and they've taken the ropes off—you realize he's no pet. He's a huge bear. It was scary. The man starts to walk down toward us, and the bear starts to walk after him, and the man turns this way, and suddenly, there's the bear. You had that bear, the camera going, and I could feel my heart thump. And then the bear turns and just goes on.

"One day we're filming a shot, 'the bear in the stream.' So the bear's sitting there in the stream, and all of a sudden he looks down, and I see him roar and grab something. Oh Jesus, he's got a muskrat or a raccoon, he's got something there. He looks like he's caught a little animal. Ohhhh! Arrrrgh. But what he's caught is his paw. He's looked in the water, the water is wrinkled, distorted, and it makes his paw look like it's moving, so he grabs his paw, pulls it up, and takes three bites out of it before he realizes it's his paw he's chewing."

Another shot called for the man and bear to amble up a slanting log. The whole crew stood below, shooting up. Unfortunately the bark was rotten, and it gave way. "The bear fell off the log. He came down with such a crash, boy, we all took off and ran in fifty directions. All I could think is, this bear is hurt, and he's gonna be furious. I'm not going to wait and see. You know what the bear did? He just sat there and sucked in air and patted his chest. The fall had knocked the breath out of him. But the ad manager for Hamm's jumped out of the way and fell over a twelve-foot cliff and broke his leg."

Of course, what you see in the final commercial are pretty pictures—the bear in a canoe, the bear in a jeep, the bear padding behind the man. The bear follows the man because he drops marshmallows out of his pantsleg, but we never see the marshmallows, or the bear vomit, or the ad manager's broken leg. What we see is a big mug of beer in a bar, with Hamm's written in neon in the window, or the bear loping back and forth on a tether, waiting for his owner to bring back two crates of Hamm's beer. And then there's the jingle, the only words in the commercial:

If you're looking for a beer that's born wet and clear,
Born in the land of sky-blue waters,
Then reach for a Hamm's, reach for a Hamm's,
Hamm's Beer is the beer you've been looking for,
Hamm's is the beer you've been looking for,
Hamm's, the beer you've been looking for,
Reach for a Hamm's, reach for a Hamm's,
Hamm's, the beer you've been looking for.

Marce Mayhew, creative director at Bozell & Jacobs, New York, has big ideas, too. He does not think much of slick execution or beauty shots. "For me, the idea is almost everything. The implementation of the idea is almost secondary." But sometimes this reckless love for a big idea can lead to a crash-landing.

In 1975 Mayhew was working for MG; except for minor cosmetic changes, the basic car had not changed in eight years. "We had handled the MG account since 1963, and they never had the budget for network TV, but now the dealers agreed that they would kick in their co-op ad dollars so we could put them on TV. So because we had taken a couple million dollars out of their pockets, we had to make a blockbuster. The client said, 'I want you to make a commercial that is not only good on the airwaves but is good enough to make the dealers stand up on their feet and applaud at the dealer meeting.' That's a hell of an assignment; that's almost a frightening assignment," says Mayhew. "Think of it. These are pretty tough guys. A car salesman—you can't do much to hoodwink one of them.

"I had had this idea cooking in the back of my head for a long time; I had tried to sell it at one time or another, but I'd never gotten to first base. So I worked up these drawings, and I went back to them, and I said, 'I think I've got a commercial that's gonna make your dealers stand up and applaud.' And they said, 'Great, let us see it.' And I said, 'Well, I can't really show it to you because it's tough to describe.' The idea: we throw an MG out of an airplane.

"It's a thirty-second commercial. You open up, you see a guy inside an airplane, and he has a helmet on. And the side of the helmet has an MG on it.   We establish the guy's in an airplane from the sound, rrrr. He looks out the window, and we see the ground. We cut, and we see three cars down there, the Fiat 124—it's the competition—the Porsche 914, and the Datsun 240 C, which is somewhat in the ballpark, one of the newer entries into the market. The Datsun and the Porsche were newer cars than the MGB. You look and you see the cars racing through this mountain road, one behind another, leaving dust trails behind them. Cut back to the guy in the plane. He gets up out of his seat and walks back in the plane, and we see the rear of the plane is open; it's a cargo plane, and an MG is parked there. He pushes it out the rear door.

"And as he pushes it out, he jumps out behind it and freefalls. The chute opens up behind the MG, a giant chute—this is all in theory now. I was describing this to the client. The car is close to the ground, the guy opens his chute, they land simultaneously, he takes off his chute, takes the rig off the MG, gets in and drives away, gets in front of those three cars, waves, and the last words are, 'MG, still one jump ahead.' It's a visual joke."

How come he wanted to spend all that money for one idea? "Commercials should be strong, powerful thirty-second stories, I think. Now slice-of-life commercials are fine—the little boy walking downstairs, seeing Daddy as Santa. I mean, that's cute, but that's not my bag. I prefer David Lean productions; they're exciting, and the viewer remembers them."

Once Mayhew got the go-ahead from MG, he had to find a producing crew. No one throws cars out of planes, so no one was an expert. Mayhew talked the English air force into cooperating, since MG is an English company, and the Israelis offered one of their planes if the production were filmed in Israel. But foreign locations cost too much. And the networks, which censor all TV advertising, added to his problems. "It was like plotting World War III. Every time I'd ask one of these production guys to bid on the job, he'd say, 'Now wait a minute, you mean the car has to be real; we can't have a fake car?' And I'd say, 'No, it has to be a real car; not only that, there has to be gasoline in the gas tank, it has to have a battery in it with acid in it, and it has to be able to start when it gets on the ground without any touch-up.' The FTC insisted on that. We showed them the story on drawing boards, and they said, 'Gee, you're implying when that thing lands that the car is so rugged it can start up.' That's exactly what they said: there's an implication in this commercial that this car is very strong to sustain that kind of impact and still drive away. I said, 'No, I don't think that was intended.' The idea was, well, a visual pun: MG is one jump ahead. That's all we were saying. So there we were: gasoline, acid in the battery, no support on the shock system. The car lands at twelve miles an hour. When you put a tank down, you see, that's something else—you can't break a tank.

"We had the National Aeronautics and Space Administration help us work out the configuration of the parachute. How much chute do you need to hold up a car? A million little details. The jumpmaster, who was in control of the chute, was an ex-military guy, and he said, 'Listen, this is under my direct control, not under your director. When I start rigging that thing to the point where it floats down, it's my thing. Then it's yours—landing.' I said, 'OK, it's a deal.' He said, 'Now there's going to be some hard, fast rules. Like: If the surface winds are

over five miles an hour at the shoot, it's a scrub.'
'Yeah, but I got a lot of money tied up; it's
twenty thousand dollars a day.' He said, 'I know,
but I gotta make that decision.' So I said, 'OK.'
He said, 'The best time to shoot is at dawn.' And
we had to go some place in the California
desert to get a big landing area because you
don't know where it's going to come down. We'd
be out at three o'clock in the morning working
under the headlights, at a place called El Mirage.
It's near Edwards Air Force Base; it's where they
had the touchdown for the space shuttle.

"So there we are. Dawn, gentlemen, start your
engines. I had two chase Cessnas out there and
a cargo plane and a helicopter. The main camera
was on the helicopter with what's called a Tyler
rig. That's a gyroscopic mount for a 35mm camera; regardless of the plane's machinations, you
can still keep your picture steady. One Cessna
had a camera; the other Cessna was above the
cargo plane so that if the guy who pushed the

car out dove too fast and passed the car, I would
have a second jumper from the plane above drop
like a rock, parallel to the car, and he would
become the actor at that point.

"So dawn starts to break. I'm ticking off the
time because at dawn the wind starts kicking
up; inside of my ear, I could feel the breeze, and
I said, 'Oh, oh, I can feel that air.' It's very still
out there in the dawn. So I said to the director,
Jim Jordan, 'Jim, let's get going. Everything's
rigged, cars in position, cameras ready.' We had
cameras all over the place: cameras in the Cessnas, two cameras over the door of the cargo
plane so we can see the guy pushing the MG
out, looking straight down so we can see the
car dropping, and you see him dropping. I had
two cameras mounted in the cockpit of the MG
so we'd be looking up at the chute when it
popped, because I wanted that footage, that
puff because I had the letters MGB on it. So Jim
said, 'Yeah, just five minutes working on some

playing with cameras, because you can't tell people there's a rotor broken in the copter. They'd go crazy. So we kept waiting and waiting and fussing, saying 'Hey, Charlie, will you check the rigging on that?' Stuff like that. So finally a plane appears in the sky and lands in the lake; he's got the rotor; they run over to the copter, jam the rotor in, and *caroooom!* The copter starts up. Now the sun is all the way up, the wind is holding off, and we go up.

"The planes get up and climb toward eight thousand feet, but that takes a long time because these cargo planes climb in a lazy circle. Finally they get up to eight thousand and they do pass-bys, dropping smoke bombs to see how much drift there is. So after three passes we establish the drift is going to be about two and a half miles to the northeast of the drop point. We're on the ground, and I've got a walkie-talkie, and I'm talking to the director, who's in the plane, and he asks me, 'Everyone down there ready?' And I say, 'This is the real thing. Let's do it. Ten, nine, eight, seven, six, five, four, three, two, one.

" 'Do it!' They push it out. I'm looking up with the binoculars. First, a drogue chute comes out the back. It opens in a series of puffs. If you put that chute out already open, it'd tear all the shroud lines right off, because the slip stream is one hundred and fifty miles an hour. This is all in theory. Beautiful. Didn't happen. The car went eight thousand feet straight into the ground. The chute did not open.

"When the MG hit the ground it compacted to about two and a half feet high, full width and full length. It was like it was a coffee table all of a sudden. It would have been great to chrome it and put a piece of glass over it. The wheels were kind of bent in. Beautiful thing.

"That was Take One. We had a contract with the production house for two drops. I'd insisted on two because I didn't think I could get it all in one shot—too many things happening—and

of the rigging on the chute.' I said, 'OK.' Five minutes later I say, 'Come on, let's go, I can feel the air, it's getting bright, let's get those things up.'

"So Jim says, 'I got bad news for you.'

" 'What's wrong? Everything looks OK.'

" 'The helicopter went to start the engine and a rotor busted.' One chance in a million. He says, 'What's happening is I got a guy racing across the desert, and he's calling Los Angeles, and there's a plane coming out with a rotor.' So we didn't dare tell the client, or anyone else. Just he and I knew this, plus one of the crew, and some guy in L.A. So we danced around,

FIAT Remy Julienne drives over a waterfall to prove he has confidence in himself and in Fiat. Then, on page 21, he does cartwheels downhill.

I wanted two for intercutting. In Take Two I was going to shoot from a different viewpoint. We only got one more drop, and we only got one car left. The client wasn't happy about losing a car because they were both for the auto show in Los Angeles—the only models in the country. So now there was only one car left in the country. But I tell the client, 'Look, if we cancel it now, the production house still has the right to charge us for the whole shoot.' I said, 'I would recommend doing Take Two because the savings aren't going to be half if we quit now.' So they said go ahead and do it.

"Assessing the damage, we suddenly realized the acid in the car had eroded the shroud lines. So it meant rerigging the parachute. We had to scrub and shoot the day after. The guys found a large hangar where we could deploy the thing and restring it. Rethink the platform. So we had a wrecked chute, a failure, a client who was not very happy, and only one car left and no assurance it would work the second try—no assurance at all. We might end up with matching coffee tables.

"We went back to Los Angeles to regroup. Meantime the guys are working overnight. They get done, and Wednesday night the guy driving the truck with the MG is on the Los Angeles freeway; he'd been awake for forty-eight hours; he fell asleep and went off the highway. Got a phone call that the guy had crashed. Luckily the MG wasn't damaged. It had been bolted down. So we got the MG out of there. Finally about two A.M. Thursday we got out there on the desert.

"At five in the morning we have breakfast out on location. Caterer comes in with coffee and sandwiches. It's very cold, and everybody eats but me; I was too harassed, running around. Dawn comes up, and we're ready to go, and I find everybody's lying around sick. They had ptomaine poisoning. One guy had a Cadillac El Dorado, and they are all in there shivering, be-cause food poisoning is very much like the flu—they shake, and they get hot. My director, my key cameraman, everybody.

"OK, I'll take over. We put another camera-man on the Tyler rig. I did the director's job. So we went ahead. The planes go up, drop their smoke bombs, the car comes out, the puff opens, the guy comes out behind it. But the drift is not what we thought. It's not going to land in the desert.

"We're below in a truck with the camera, so we get these cars going, and we all drive at eighty miles an hour, because we want to get to the touchdown point, to get the landing sequence. It's two and a half miles away. We had the pedal to the metal, screaming across the desert.

"We just get there in time. But there's big cactus all over. It's lumpy ground, too, no longer flat. We can only hope that mother lands right. If it lands on top of a cactus, that's our second car. *Bam.* It just lands in the only place that's smooth.

"We get footage of the car landing, the guy landing, and we got a commercial. Almost. The thing was: I didn't get the footage I really wanted, but the concept was so strong, so dynamic, that the slickness of the photography wasn't missing. Despite the fact that we only had one take, we had a commercial because we got that idea."

The result: A commercial in which we seem to fall out of the plane with the car, sail down, thump into the ground, then race out ahead of the competition. No one got hit on the head; the ptomaine poisoning cleared up; the client sold cars.

Sometimes when a really first-rate disaster occurs on a set, the writer may put it into the commercial. Amil Gargano, a partner in Ally & Gargano, had done a number of stunts with Remy Julienne jumping a Fiat from one building to another, from a road onto a barge, demon-

strating how tough the little car is. "When you have a man who has been doing these stunts for fourteen years, and he keeps trying to exceed himself each time, he's doing some pretty risky things. He told me some new ideas. He said he could drive a car over a waterfall."

Gargano sent out a team scouting waterfalls in France. The one they found was an eighteen-foot drop. "The falls must have been a hundred and fifty feet across. This was in the mountains of the Southern Alps, about two hours northeast of Nice. It was a sheer drop, ninety degrees at the top, ninety degrees at the bottom, no slope, because this was a man-made wall that the water was tumbling over. What we had to do was construct a forty-five-degree ramp at the base of the falls so the car could continue driving after it got over. What we had to do first, of course, was to divert all the water in the stream. We had two bulldozers come in and move all the water by filling up the banks. We had a crew of fifty working seven days a week, really knocking themselves out preparing this ramp under the waterfall. And then a huge storm came and washed the ramp out about two weeks before we were to shoot, wiped out a crane, almost lost a bulldozer; it washed the driver right out of the cab. Here I am going for seven seconds of film—and all these people, all this effort!

"Finally they got the new ramp constructed; the bulldozers rediverted the water so that it was coming down over our ledge, and we started shooting. Julienne was going to drive over the falls and then continue as far as he could before he got hung up on the rocks in the stream. So he went over the waterfall, and he ended up upside down. About eight seconds later he came bobbing up out of the water, saying 'I'm sorry, but my timing was a little off.' What happened was this: he came over the waterfall, and the car's nose hit the ramp and his forward momentum flipped the car over so the car ended up on its roof and stayed that way. We hauled the car up the side of the cliff with a bulldozer, and it got pretty banged up because they had a hard time turning it over in the water. And then Julienne said, 'I think I could do it again.' And I said, 'Can you do it in this car?' And he said, 'Yes, I think so. I don't see any problem; it's just a matter of flushing the engine, changing the plugs, and putting in new oil; if there was any damage to the car, it's mostly to the roof.' So I said, 'Well, let's do it.' So the car was sent to Nice, the engine was flushed, new oil was put in, new plugs were put in, and about two days later we had four motion picture cameras and four still cameras all in position. And it looks a little like demolition derby, because there's no windshield on the car. And he did the thing beautifully. He came over, and it was fantastic.

"In my mind while we were redoing the thing, I rewrote the script, and when I came back, I refined it some more. It became a thirty-second commercial, whereas it was supposed to be only a seven-second segment in a commercial. Now it has Remy Julienne saying, 'My name is Remy Julienne. I'm a professional stunt driver; despite all my care and planning, I will make the slightest error in timing, and the stunt will fail. So we haul the car out of the water, put in new plugs, new oil, and we try it again. I believe in myself. I believe in Fiat.' "

The truth in a commercial! Now that's courage, to film your own car going tail pipe over roof, upending in the drink, and then to show it on the air. Neat writing, too, to turn what could have been a drowning into a pitch for Fiat.

a man jumps out of a plane and his watch falls off. It drops thousands of feet to a grassy field. An hour later he and his buddy find it: yes, it's still ticking. It's a Timex.

Regular TV programs stab, mutilate, and kill people, and their ratings go up. Commercials hurt products—and tests show audiences watch extra-carefully.

"You get them any way you can," says Jerry Della Femina, the adman who looks like Kojak on a diet. "I'm sure in the Timex commercials people get off on seeing the Timex get beat up. You don't look at your Timex, you first get a gorilla to punch it, rap it around, stomp on it, drop it out the window, then you look at it and say, 'Gee, it's terrific, the time is . . . exactly.' And it's still running."

Perhaps audiences secretly enjoy watching products—so often praised—get torn to shreds on TV. Certainly we have reasons to resent those glossy Goody Two-shoes of TV: Since products are usually presented as perfectly splendid by shockingly healthy models in clean kitchens, such commercials may make us feel imperfect and second-rate. A natural reaction would be to punch the product. Also, the people who threaten, coax, and persuade us to use the product often resemble our mothers, fathers, or grandparents, and part of our minds may begin to equate the product with baths, galoshes, and spinach ordered by these authorities in childhood; subconsciously we may come to think of many products as good for us, but hateful. Even if we feel bullied into buying a deodorant, we may still feel tricked or pressured, and long to see the can explode.

Our hostility isn't only touched off by the way commercials are presented, either. The cakewalk of new products during a commercial break reminds us that we cannot afford to buy them; if we are suffering from middle-class wallets, we may resent each new temptation to spend. Furthermore, any new product that disappoints us

adds to the deep-seated mistrust of untested products. We have been promised that something will work, and then it fails; why shouldn't we take a vicarious pleasure in watching the product get smashed? Remember, as a child, whomping a toy car you had broken and saying, "Bad car!"? Thus commercials that put products through the torture test, supposedly to prove their strength, may appeal to people's unconscious hunger for revenge.

From the evidence of sixty years of movies, Americans like watching violence. The TV programs themselves offer us enough massacres to excite the most bloodthirsty among us; commercials hide this violence by directing it against objects. By mauling the product rather than an announcer (which do you hate more?), an advertiser allows us to enjoy violence without feeling guilty about people getting hurt.

Commercials would be very different if this violence were to become as overt as it is in programs. When *Mad* magazine imagined regular TV programs using the Timex scenario, for example, they created a Mr. Asmus who had to go through the waterproof test *with* his watch. First, two fire trucks blast his glasses off. He ends up panting and dripping like a victim on *Emergency* or *C.H.I.P.S.* Then there's the shock test, in which two hard hats pound him on the head with sledgehammers. In the antimagnetic test, a huge crane with an electromagnet lifts him up by his suspender buttons, then drops him in front of the announcer, who says, "Powerful, eh? And now . . . finally, the dirt test! Yes, a real torture test." Fourteen tons of dirt and gravel slide out of a dump truck on top of Mr. Asmus as if Starsky and Hutch were at the controls. Only his hand flops out. Sure enough, his Timeless watch is still ticking—and it's still ticking in the next frame, where Mr. Asmus is hauled away under a white sheet.

In one hour of regular TV programming in 1976 there were about 9.5 incidents of physical force intended to hurt or kill a human being, according to studies made by the American Medical Association; cartoons average twenty-two such incidents an hour. Their definition of violence is broader than that of the network censors, who review scripts for each show before they're OK'd for airing: network censors tend to overlook violence if it's part of a good joke, an accident, or an Act of God, like an earthquake. But even so the CBS censors allow three incidents of interpersonal violence per hour outside the family hour. Compared to these programs, commercials, are Red Cross nurses. Commercials rarely mangle people. And if anyone suffers in a commercial, the announcer comes on with medicine for fast, fast relief.

To hear them tell it, ad agencies now lead such pure lives that some even advise their clients not to advertise on the high-casualty-rate shows, no matter how many viewers tune in. In the late Sixties a wave of popular protest against television violence began to be expressed in letters written to the networks about the U.S. "war machine" and its cultural support systems, including television. Admen ignored the letters, but in the early Seventies protesters banded together in groups like Action for Children's Television, and the complaints about bloody programs began to take on a prim, middle-class tone, complete with quotes from Freud and the Bible. In addition, research done by ad agency J. Walter Thompson showed that as many as ten percent of the people it surveyed "had considered not buying a product because it had been advertised on a program they considered excessively violent," and eight percent actually avoided such purchases: Thompson executives concluded that violence in programming might

TIMEX   One of a series of testimonials from people whose Timex watches survived casual or brutal treatment.

SERGEANT ALLCHIN: We were flying at 2500 feet in a C47

My Timex watch got yanked off my wrist,

until to our surprise we found my Timex,

on a parachute jump.

I pulled the cord.

(SOUND OF PARACHUTE OPENING)

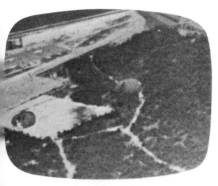

800 feet in the air.

After I hit the ground,

my buddy and I searched for an hour,

and it was still ticking.

So Timex, I wonder if other watches could take that much.

ANNOUNCER: Timex. It takes a licking and keeps on ticking.

hurt sales of products advertised during the show. Oscar Mayer, the bacon and frankfurter company, says it wants its ads to be "a guest in the house"; Johnson & Johnson baby products has pulled out of forty shows in the last two years to avoid being smeared with stray violence; and Kimberly-Clark has issued press releases refusing to sponsor "unwarranted violence and anti-social behavior." Kraft enunciates the Velveeta-type programming they dream of: "interesting but not intrusive, exciting but not offensive, provocative but not antagonistic." It sounds like American food.

Samsonite luggage is another advertiser that opposes shows with "excessive violence, sex, or matters of poor taste," which is odd because Samsonite let the Pittsburgh Steelers toss around their suitcases and purses, jump on them, block them, tackle them, toss them, and pile up on top of them to prove that Samsonite luggage lasts. What about violence to products? Even though the agencies have kept from hurting humans too often, they seem to spend a lot of money and energy hurting their own products—and their own names.

Western Electric, for example, shows beautiful pictures of its own machines knocking hell out of phones, jiggling them, rattling them, dropping them. It's supposed to prove the phones can survive even an average American kid.

And Timken blasts its own steel thirty different ways to show how strong its alloys are in a

These men break concrete sidewalks all day long, so you know they're really hitting **hard!**

© 1974 by Dick de Bartolo, Angelo Torres and E. C. Publications, Inc.

MAD *Mad Magazine* shows what would happen if torture tests were done during television programs: the wearer would get hit, along with his watch. (*left*) CONTINENTAL INSURANCE We start with a foot that kicks a skate that swings a door that hits a vase that tips a plant that pushes a light, knocking over a picture, a table, a radio, scaring a dog who bumps a chair that shoves a piano right through the flimsy wall of the client's house. Luckily, he's insured. And only the house got hurt. (*opposite*)

Prepared by Doyle Dane Bernbach for The Continental Insurance Group

fast, visually fascinating commercial produced at Dolphin Computer Animation. A red column of swirling ribbons appears. "When we test Timken alloy steel, we put it through the mill." The ribbons become letters spelling S T E E L. They turn shiny gray. "We can stretch it" (the centers of the letters sag, the ends get higher), "crack it" (a slash of black rips through the letters), "crush it" (they become shrunken and wrinkled), "heat it to 2400 degrees above" (red glows around the shaking letters), "and freeze it to 320 degrees below" (a blue light emerges behind each part of the letters), "inspect it ultrasonically" (a grid appears in back and a jagged yellow line charts a graph through the letters), "fluoroscopically" (they fill with purple liquid),

"then we test it some more." (Red rays scan below. The S and L rise up, and electricity arcs between them.) "Up to thirty tests in all, just to make sure that . . ." (here sections are removed from the top, like slabs) ". . . we made our steel bars and tubes just right. Nobody's tougher on Timken steel than the Timken company." Somehow, perhaps because we don't see any real banging or pouring or crushing, the effect of this tough-talking commercial is elegant, safe, and even pretty.

The problem with product torture tests—especially animated ones—is that people may not believe them. In the interests of credibility, the Master Lock Company set up a test anyone can duplicate. They hired an expert marksman, Jim

Bell, and rented the Angeles Shooting Range, out in Little Tujunga Canyon in San Fernando, California. There they bolted their ten-buck Master No. 15 Super Security Padlock on a red and white target. Bell brought his .308 Mauser 98 Action rifle, with a Douglas Premium Grade Barrel and a Lyman 20 Power Scope, paced off forty yards, and, when the lights and reflectors and sound lines necessary for the commercial were ready, shot the lock. The 150-grain bullet blasted a half-inch hole through the center of the padlock, but the lock did not open. They shot it again, and it still did not open. All this they got down on film—and thus began a nationwide orgy of violence to Master Locks.

To prove the lock's survival was not a fluke, Bell went ahead and shot up thirty-nine more locks. Of forty locks, only one opened on the first shot, and only three more opened on the second shot. Master Lock showed the commercial on the 1977 Super Bowl show, and two journalists who saw it tried to duplicate the results on their own. Harry Haigley of the *Miami News* hired Medero Garcias, a local marksman, to use his deer rifle on the lock. Unfortunately they could only use the National Rifle and Pistol Range, which is much shorter than the range Bell had used; so Garcias paced 15 yards closer to his target than Bell had been and squeezed off a shot. "The bullet went into the heart of the lock, but not through it," Haigley reported. "The lock would not open, as was shown on TV." Garcias shot again and managed to hit the same spot. "The second bullet did not destroy it to the point that it could be pulled open." Haigley pointed out that the demonstration proved two things: "First, the next time you see a detective or cowboy show and someone pulls a gun and blasts open a lock on a door, you know it is only make-believe. Big, modern-day locks simply cannot be opened that way; also, they send out a dangerous spray of metal fragments when hit by a bullet. Second, it shows that Master Locks are pretty tough."

Nashville, Tennessee, police found the same thing. At the request of the Nashville *Banner*, Officer Ken Pence, a marksman with the Metro Unusual Situation Team (a MUST, not a SWAT), put five shots into the same-model lock, and it still would not open. A $1.50 model they tried also held, but the cop said you could probably open the cheaper one with a crowbar after all that damage.

In 1974 Tonka Toys showed an elephant resting one foot on a Tonka truck without ruining it. And *Consumer Reports* tested this out. "Although our test equipment doesn't include pachyderms, we subjected both trucks to a thousand pounds of mechanical force over the cab-shield—

AMERICAN TOURISTER   In this spot we see a dramatic re-creation of seven incidents in which tourists dropped their luggage out of their cars and found that the suitcases survived.

the same spot the elephant used for a footrest. The metal bent and the tires deflated temporarily, but the toys were still usable." And in France, Samsonite hired an elephant to snatch a man's bag off his head, drag it, drop it, and threaten to sit on it.

Not to be bested by its competitor Samsonite, American Tourister created a whole series of ads in which they knock around their own suitcases. In one, the announcer writes a love letter to horrible people: "Dear clumsy bellboys, brutal cab drivers, careless doormen, ruthless porters, savage baggage masters, and all butter-fingered luggage handlers all over the world. Have we got a suitcase for you!" While these words are spoken,

we see a gorilla approach a suitcase, pick it up, leap up to a bar with it, sit on it, drop it, and drag it back into his cage. American Touristers have been used as jacks: the J. C. Quinly family of Walnut Creek, California, had jacked up their car to change a flat and left the suitcase right behind the rear bumper. Suddenly the car rolled backward off the jack and fell onto the suitcase, which held the car up. American Tourister admits, "Of course, the suitcase got dented," but Mr. Quinly fixed the dent in the suitcase with a hammer.

The ultimate American Tourister hit-and-run accident was created in 1976 when Doyle Dane Bernbach roped off a stretch of highway, rented

ANNOUNCER: Robert Ammon, Michigan, Mrs. James Simonds, New Hampshire, Mrs. Frank O'Brien, Alabama, Mrs. Travis Wiginton, California, Robert Geroy, North Carolina, James Edelstein, Wisconsin, Mrs. D. M. Olson, Minnesota . . . Ask them whether an American Tourister is a great suitcase to have . . . when you hit the road.

Prepared by Doyle Dane Bernbach for American Tourister Luggage

a gigantic semitrailer, and made a little movie: the truck comes over the hill in early morning sunlight and wisps of fog. We hear its horn. We see the painted panels in front, the headlights, and we pull back to see that the truck is about to hit—yes—an American Tourister suitcase. *Wham.* The suitcase flies through the air. Another crash, and we see the suitcase land. A man appears from nowhere and opens the suitcase. His clothes are in perfect order. He reaches down inside the clothes and pulls out an egg. To prove it's not broken, he cracks it and lets the yolk fall on his suitcase. The voice-over pitch: "American Tourister would like to remind you that the reason we make our suitcases so strong isn't just to protect our suitcases. It's to help protect what's inside our suitcases." Crashes must work: over the nine years of the campaign, American Tourister's dollar shipments have increased geometrically, and during the period of the egg-and-truck commercial, they sold more units than in any year before.

Traditionally, torture tests show you that one brand of tire can last no matter what it runs over. For Firestone, three men in a truck toss boards, glass, and rocks out the back while a car with Sup-R-Belt Tires catches up and zooms past them. The announcer keeps muttering, "Strong cord for extra long mileage, strong sidewalls for extra long mileage, strong bonding for extra long mileage." Sears takes its Steel-Belted Radials onto the Sahara desert as part of its "Tough Roads of the World Campaign." The announcer: "There are still some places in the world where people seldom see a car. Where they don't worry about what roads do to an automobile." We see camels, and the car comes out of a slough kicking dust; it bounces all four wheels off the road; it swivels through a landscape of six-inch rocks. The logic in these commercials is off: how many Americans will drive over the Atlas Mountains next year? But Ford caught on in 1977. They plugged the Fairmont by showing it on local rough roads; in New York it navigated the Second Avenue washboard, with all its patches and potholes; people identified with the locale and the treatment and bought the car.

And then there was the Studebaker that Mobil took up onto the roof of a ten-story building. Mobil wanted to show what can happen to a car in a head-on collision that has the force of a drop from ten stories up. Adman Terry Galanoy remembers, "The agency bought the old car, had it hoisted to the top of a ten-story building, and then threw it off. It made quite a dent in the street and in the history of television commercials." Did part of the appeal of this commercial come from the sight of a usually shiny product taking a beating?

Cars seem to bring out the destructive impulse in Americans. Charlie Moss once created a campaign for American Motors' Javelin that was so destructive it upset even the torturers. In it, a wrecking crew approaches a Mustang, each hard hat carrying angle irons, crowbars, and screwdrivers. An announcer ponders philosophically, "If you started out with this basic idea for a sporty car..." But then the workers rip off a bumper. "Then added heavier contour bumpers...." They smash the windows with a wrecking ball. "And wildly extravagant no-vent windows...." We see the cloth seat covers slashed. And as the announcer tells us the car is going to be made bigger, we see pipes pulled out, the engine thrown away, and finally, the car blown up. He whistles. Having destroyed the competitor's Mustang, the construction crew walks in with the new Javelin.

The competition—Ford—was annoyed, and even the sponsor, American Motors, was surprised. They asked Moss how come. He said, "People don't know what a Javelin is. We should tell them what a Javelin is. We need an area of reference. The Javelin is like a Mustang. But it is better. So we take a Mustang apart—with

hammers and saws and torches—and show how we would build that car in a better way. That better car is called a Javelin."

As it turned out, this commercial helped sell both Javelins and Mustangs, and Ford was not nearly so upset about it as was Chevrolet. They were put out because American Motors had used a Mustang; they felt that a Camaro would have given the comparison much more quality.

Often the violence or threat of violence in a commercial seems like the acting out of the audience's suppressed fears. There's another Javelin spot that does this, bringing our fear of rip-offs and muggings out into the open and laughing at it. The set looks like *West Side Story*: brownstones, tough teenaged punks hanging out. The hoods trot over to a new Javelin. The leader says, "They tell me this car Javelin is priced lower than other sporty cars. Well, I know my cars, and you could have fooled me. I mean, you take those bumpers—not now, stupid." (Here he stops a gang member who is trying to boost one.) The leader praises the car, and each gang member gets to chime in for one element. (Kid under the hood: "Two-thirty-two cube on a six-pack, seventeen bearing crank, all synchromesh gearbox, hey, you got a car!") Leader concludes: "So in conclusion I can honestly say this new Javelin has got everything we look for in a car." It looks like they're going to steal it. But a fat man in a T-shirt comes out of one of the brownstones: "Hey, punks, get away from that car." Encouraging kids to steal your car? No, says the agency, Wells, Rich, Greene. "It does no more to encourage crime than the programming it is in."

Perhaps the most aesthetically planned act of violence to a product was conceived and orchestrated by that David Lean of creative men, Marce Mayhew of Bozell & Jacobs. Having turned one MG into a coffee table, Mayhew moved on to Minolta cameras. He was not trying to prove that they are tough, merely that they had created a new camera by taking apart two previously distinct cameras—the sophisticated 35mm Single Lens Reflex camera and the cartridge-loading 110 pocket camera. Barbara Lobron, who worked on this account with Mayhew, says, "Finding a way to illustrate graphically that the Minolta 110 Zoom SLR represents the best of both worlds for picture-takers posed quite a challenge." They decided to blow up the two cameras and reassemble them as the new one— although to achieve that effect what they would do was to blow up a Minolta 110 SLR and then run the film backwards.

"It was totally unpredictable," says Mayhew. "We had no idea how those fragments were going to blow. As an artist, I'm concerned with the explosion just as an explosion, but it has to be a beautiful explosion. The idea was strong enough, so we felt if we could even get it close to what we wanted, well, we'd have the commercial.

"We ended up not using dynamite. We used compressed air. It can be very highly charged, six hundred pounds per square inch. We put a little air jet under where the camera was sitting and got the compression up to six hundred pounds; we just said, 'Blow it!' And *boom*. So the air direction is more controllable. We had our special effects man Alfred Denda prescore the camera and take out the screws. The body was weakened so it would break at the right spot. Lens rings came apart. Talcum powder for smoke. Very sophisticated. The backlighting made it look like smoke because there was so much light there.

"The logistics of that commercial were incredible. The entire thing was shot at twenty-five hundred frames per second. A normal movie is twenty-four frames a second, which is a lot of image being recorded. We were recording twenty-five hundred images a second. We had to have a special camera sent in from California; there is only one camera like this held by a private company—the rest are owned by the military for ballistic studies. They're the fastest movie cameras around. Big as a table. You have a five-hundred-foot roll of film; it took two hundred and fifty feet of that film just to get the camera up to speed. Camera's like a car; it has an acceleration process. *Rrrr*. There's a tachometer; you see the needle go up to where you want it to be. The compressor has to be up to pressure

MINOLTA Minolta blows up a camera and, by running the film backwards, makes the parts seem to reassemble, creating a new model.

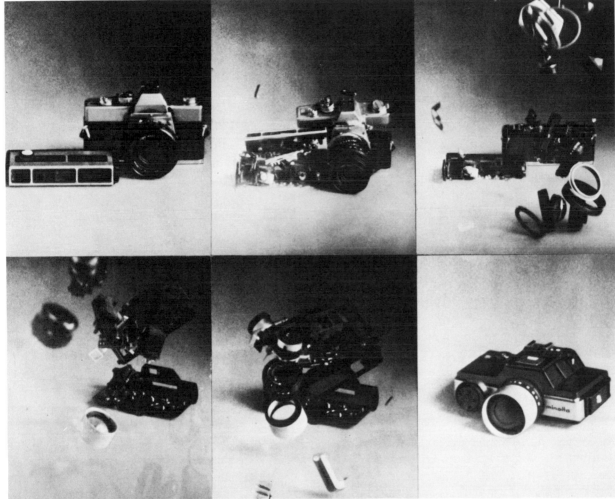

Credit: Minolta

at the same time. Another problem is how much light you have to have. With most cameras even one-thousandth of a second requires a great deal of light to get a meter reading, and here we were recording each frame at one/twenty-five-hundredth of a second per exposure. So we had to pump in an incredible amount of light, tungsten. To light it artistically was impossible. You couldn't even look at the thing without welder's goggles on. In twenty-five seconds the camera began to warp. You could see it melting.

"Lights had to be full intensity at the time the camera's up to speed and the compression's up to pressure. You yell, 'Speed—fire!' And then *bang*. And as soon as we got the take, we said, 'Kill the lights.'

"The explosion lasted thirty-four milliseconds. It was shrapnel. We had a plywood wall with a hole window to see the action. Everything was contained inside the plywood container.

"That's the way I like to think of commercials. It was an incredible selling success. People walk into a store, and they don't necessarily remember the name of the camera, or the brand, or the number of it; they'll say they want the camera that explodes. They love the concept of the 110 SLR with the zoom lens. They call it the camera that explodes. In fact, it's the one that comes back together again. I guess I just like unpredictable events."

Unpredictable for him. Profitable for Minolta. And fun for us. Perhaps our consumer culture—and the usually hyperpositive commercials for products—have nourished in each of us a certain resentment at all those shiny "goods" on TV. The advertiser who dares mess up his own car attracts us—and gives us real pictures of events we could only have dreamt before. These ads don't necessarily prove that the product is tough; but they entertain us, letting us enjoy our own rage for destruction.

But commercials prevent us from becoming too conscious of our violent impulses. They claim they are doing this for higher reasons—to prove the car, the tire, the suitcase is well-built, strong, long-lasting. So our mind can excuse the slam-bang by calling it "a test," or a "proof." The trappings of logic and science help us pretend we watch just because we are curious consumers.

What our unconscious wants, TV gives us. On television programs we get to see people throttled, drowned, electrocuted, stabbed, garroted, punched, stomped, run over, cemented to death, knocked off skyscrapers, blown up in cars, burned by eerie rays, and blasted to invisibility by cosmic ants—not to mention kidnapped, raped, tortured, and blackmailed. After all this is it any wonder that some of us long to lash out with a hit or a kick? Then comes a commercial, which tells us we can grind our dishwasher, strip our tires, put our locks through hell, blow up our cameras, run over our suitcases—and our announcer encourages us to act on these replacements, these substitutes for real people.

Numerous studies show that watching *Starsky & Hutch, Baretta,* and *Charlie's Angels* leads people to believe that society is more violent than it is. We have little defense against programs that mimic reality and make us believe they mirror it. But with commercials we can always draw back from belief, dismissing the spot as "just an ad"—we always know the point of a commercial is to get our attention and sell. The ultimate illustration of this truth is the story of what happened when one ad writer decided to send a new brand of peanut butter up in a hot-air balloon guided by Don Piccard. Unfortunately the pilot of the helicopter carrying the camera crew had only flown a helicopter once before. Usually he dusted crops. The helicopter's churning rotorblades got too close to the balloon and blew it over, so the hot air rushed out. The balloon began to fall. Piccard looked around for his helmet. He had forgotten it. He grabbed the nearest thing that looked like a helmet and put it on his head; it was the large metal bowl of peanut butter. Unbelievably, the thick gooeyness of the peanut butter protected his skull when the balloon banged down hard on a supermarket parking lot.

Was anyone impressed by this near disaster? "Two ladies who had just left the supermarket were wheeling their groceries by as the balloon came crashing down," reports adman Terry Galanoy in his book *Down the Tube*. " 'Don't even look at it,' one said, staring straight ahead. 'They're just trying to get your attention.' "

Every business day—in offices at the networks and at the ad business's self-regulating boards —censors protect us from seeing toilet bowls on TV. They also nix pictures of breasts, navels, genitals, urination, defecation, intercourse, oral sex, pregnant women who want to make love, two people in one bathtub, a woman sucking her own forefinger, and kisses that last more than thirty seconds. How many pleasures of real life these censors ban from the airwaves!

Consider the nipple. In Holland a jewelry salesman undresses a woman in a sunlit room, then puts his best bracelets on top of her breast, circling an erect and quite pink teat. What this has to do with jewelry advertising is anyone's guess; but in America the Television Code Authority of the National Association of Broadcasters has for years denied well-reasoned requests from Playtex and Hanes to show real flesh underneath bras. Playtex models have to wear sweaters and drape tape measures over their chests to suggest where the bras might go. In other commercials, literally disembodied bras float through space as if looking for a human. The only American commercials that show real human breasts are on *Midnight Blue,* the syndicated cable show produced by *Screw* magazine and shown on pay-TV in major hotels; from a low angle we look up at lurid girls dancing topless in front of glaring lights. They do have big breasts, and they manage to maintain a smile as they lean over the cameraman, then hustle backwards while the announcer invites you to visit a topless bar. But conventional TV remains just that—conventional.

Commercials exaggerate the ecstasy possible through use of the sponsor's product—leading us to dream of sex—but quite quickly the commercial chops off any scene that gets too hot. The result: a continual cycle of arousal and disappointment. Commercials hint at more and show less than any of the programs they sponsor. In this way these thirty-second vignettes reflect the national schizophrenia about obscenity: we want it, we feel entitled to it, but we also suffer public shame at such impulses and pretend they only last a few seconds. Hence our spots resemble massage parlors that pose as baths (dirty but clean).

"There's not enough sex in commercials," says Jerry Della Femina. "We are working our way toward becoming a sexless society, so there can't be any sex in commercials. You know, there are three people in charge of sex in the United States; they're at NBC, CBS, and ABC, the network censors. The head censor at each network is the man in charge of sex. He decides whether or not I'm old enough to see this and that. I'm forty-one and he still doesn't think I'm old enough to see sex on TV. He's in full control of sex in advertising. They get to see it. But they dole it out to us little by little: I mean we get a breast here, or a flash of a breast there. The only commercials that don't have trouble with sex are those which are absolutely obscene. A commercial that says, 'I've been stroked this morning,' or 'Great balls of lather'—now this is true obscenity. You have a sweet young thing looking into the camera saying, 'I stroke him every morning,' and the censor can't believe you mean what you said, so he lets that go. The thing he takes away is someone saying something that doesn't have anything to do with sex. He's so carefully looking for the double entendre that he can't find the single entendre. They absolutely do not see sex in advertising if it's blatant; but if you should try to do something else, they can find sex. They can find sex in a garage mechanic talking about shock absorbers. But let somebody say, 'Flick my Bic'—this is beautifully obscene—everyone nods their heads and lets that go, because it's obvious that Bic and prick and stroke, well, we know you can't possibly mean that, that would be obscene, you wouldn't come near me with that type of commercial. So the secret of success with censors is to be more

Wet your whistle.

obscene: the most obscene commercial you can find is the commercial that will be accepted.

"A toilet is a big thing for them. They are very uptight about that. I find it's best to present commercials to them late in the afternoon so their toilet problems will have been flushed in the morning; they're better people for it. But even in the afternoon they're very concerned about toilet bowls. The American people, according to them, are not involved with such things. We sell toilet bowl cleaners, but we can't show a commode. That clear glass toilet! That's the obscenity: what they get you to resort to. That little guy floating on a barge down in the toilet in **Ty-D-bol** commercials—the only reason he's in the barge is that you couldn't possibly show a commode and have a human talking about how you want to have blue water in the toilet bowl. So the agency says, OK, we'll make it very simple; we'll have a guy playing 'Lemon Tree, Lemon Tree' on the guitar because it's a

LIP QUENCHER Sultry woman, whose whistle sucks us into a moisturizer pitch, seems to be laughing at her own imitation of the sound track, "Moon River." (*above*)

FRUIT OF THE LOOM The scene: the woman's laundry room. The cast: iron-on people, who pop to life. The point: no human being can wear underwear on TV without the censors shouting foul. Result: a clean commercial. (*right*)

lemon-fragrance toilet bowl cleaner, see, and he'll be on a barge. What's so terrible about this is that years from now when we finally bomb ourselves, and we all die, and some scientist starts to find out about our culture, all they're going to find is one print of the **Ty-D-bol** commercial. It's the only thing that's going to be left. They're going to restore it, and they're going to put it on a projector, and then they are going to figure out what we were. That's where we were: floating in giant toilet bowls."

Most advertising executives are less irritated by such censorship. In fact, some worry that sexy shows may be upsetting conventional audiences, souring them for the products advertised in the wholesome commercials that follow. The Marsteller agency puts out a newsletter about supermarket products called *Checkout,* in which it has argued, "The sultry bedroom scene, complete with panting lovers, may not be the ideal occasion for interruption by a cheery breakfast food jingle." Some major corporations have set up their own standards, and, they claim, they will yank commercials off a show that has excessive sex or violence. Their trade association, the Association of National Advertisers, has told the networks that it is worried "that the former glut of violence may be followed by excessive

FRUITS: Hi, Emma!

portrayal of sex and sex-oriented jokes and/or other subjects in bad taste," and it has also warned advertisers that they can no longer insulate themselves from "program-content decisions."

Ironically, commercials may have broken TV's prudery down in the mid-Sixties. You'd have had to look sharp to find sex—or even a long kiss—on most TV during the Fifties. Carmen Miranda, maybe, on *The Ed Wynn Show,* or a couple getting too close on Dick Clark's *American Bandstand.* Par for the course was the dancing on *The Arthur Murray Party.* But beginning in the Sixties, commercials themselves started coming on strong. Gunilla Knutson, who had been Miss Sweden, told men to take it all off now with Noxema; later she commented, "It used to be the girl next door. Now they let you be sexy." Miss White Owl began breathing hard, feathering her large breasts: "There's more to a White Owl than just smoke." Slowly, network TV admitted that there was more to life than smoke screens; but even in the early 1970's the networks thought themselves very daring for bringing up such previously unmentionable facts of life as abortion, pregnancy out of wedlock, orgasms, incest, couples living together, and, finally, the existence of homosexuality. Thus,

by the mid-Seventies TV had begun naming various previously obscene things, but in general TV still avoided showing them. Words, perhaps —disapproving words, particularly—but no pictures.

Still, even the mention of such taboo thoughts as intercourse and sodomy scared audiences and aroused complaints, so the vice-presidents of the networks started giving major speeches claiming, as William Rubens said, "There isn't any sex on TV." As vice-president for research and corporate planning at NBC, Rubens argued, "Television shows couples kissing and embracing, sex is discussed in a restrained manner, and there is innuendo—but never actual sex! ... Television is not and does not want to be a trendsetter of the sexual revolution. In fact, it lags *behind* the prevailing attitudes." But if network TV is conservative, then commercials are positively reactionary. The rule-of-thumb now is: Commercials hint at what the networks show. And what the networks dare to talk about without showing, the commercials never mention.

Because the ad-makers bite their tongues so tightly, audiences sometimes may not even know what's being advertised. In commercials women do not have menstrual periods since they don't have vaginas or uteruses; so advertising tampons

EMMA: Hi yourself, cuties! Whatcha doin' in my laundry basket?

LEAF: Checking how Fruit of the Loom briefs stand up to dryer heat. Superband waistband's A.O.K.

EMMA [to APPLE]: Bet you'd make a heckuva pie, chubby.

gets tricky. One product just makes you "feel feminine fresh." Water could do as well. And men never put on underwear on TV, so Fruit of the Loom has a man open his drawer and pull out . . . no . . . it's a very fat apple, a leaf, and two sprigs of grapes which turn as if by magic into men dressed in ludicrous fruit costumes— as if they were going to a child's Halloween party. "Ahhhh! It's the little Fruit of the Loom guys from TV," says one man in the ad. They pop out and demonstrate the new Superband

waistband on a pair of men's cotton briefs. In another commercial the same crew emerge from an elderly woman's wash to point out that the Superband outlasts even tough dryer heat. The last word goes to the woman. She pokes the fat apple in the belly: "Bet you'd make a heckuva pie, chubby." We may not realize that this commercial is supposed to sell underwear—but at least it's laundered clean.

Audiences enjoy sex almost as much as violence, to judge from scores of research projects, rating charts, and sales figures. And sex sells products because people believe the basic premise that somewhere someday something they buy is going to produce a miracle; in one magic flash they will become lithe, handsome, glossy, and charming. Even if the product doesn't actually change them overnight, it will remind them, each time they use it, of that beautiful person in the commercial. As Erich Fromm said in the 1973 CBS show, "You and the Commercial," "Since there is very little love in our society, sex plays an important role." Or, as big-busted Charo says, squatting next to a car decorated by MAACO Auto Painting and Bodyworks, "Everyone likes to look at a beautiful body, no?" The association of sex—or sexiness—sells the product. "Men, take it off. Take it all off," says the starlet. What does that mean? "Well," says an adman who would rather not use his name ("Call me Carl Wrighter"), "it's supposed to mean that Noxema Shave Cream works the way a shave cream is supposed to work; you put it on, you shave it off, right? Wrong. Not when you put those words into the mouth of a six-foot blonde and have her say them as if she were ten seconds away from an orgasm. The words still mean what they mean, but, oh, so much more."

Sure. But since no overt act of sexual intercourse may take place on TV, you have to use subtler lines, jokes, sidelong glances, knowing smirks, and these double entendres often play on unconscious impulses turned up by researchers in

hours of interviews with consumers. One chain of stereo stores called Wall-to-Wall started some commercials with the line, "Please be kind. This is my first time." Martin Kramer, who worked up the commercial, says, "The double entendre wasn't thrown in to shock people. Our research showed that many men buy stereo equipment to impress women."

National Airlines found out that businessmen who fly a lot daydream about the stewardesses. Result: a series of beautiful stewardesses appealing to us, "Fly me." How would Erich Fromm analyze that commercial? "By a slight change of letters. And it's not even that unconscious. One doesn't need to be a specialist in symbolic language to see that. It is just an attempt to shift the argument completely from the value of an airline to a sexual illusion." The illusion that National's stewardesses want to fly off to a motel with their passengers was given even sharper detail in another commercial in which a bouncy blonde jumps into her sports car, slams the door, and roars off saying, "Everything they say about Miami girls is true. We're always on the move.... And I adore to fly." She reaches the beach, and walks into the sun. She turns to talk to us. "Fly to Miami, come on, any day." She unbuttons her blouse and slips off her dress. She's wearing two tiny strips of bikini, smaller than a bra and panties. She backs into the fiery glow of the Florida sun, to be replaced by another

stewardess who says, "I'm Judy. Fly me."

National tried to defend itself from charges of sexism and suggestiveness by giving all its planes names like Judy or Carol—turning the sex objects into objects. This kind of coyness can be arresting in itself, as in the Speidel digital watch commercial where a groom shocks his bride by saying, "Honey, this is the day. Today I'm going all the way." He isn't—as we learn later—talking about anything racier than buying a digital watch; our attention is hooked. The sexual sell seems most "pasted on" and perverse when it is used for products that have nothing to do with genitalia or love.

The MEM Company goes in the other direction with the most frankly sexual advertising on legitimate TV. They put smoldering women on pool tables, saying, "...All my men wear English Leather, or they wear nothing at all." In another, a woman dressed like the Miami stewardess takes off her coat, revealing a bikini underneath; she likes men who surf, and men who ski, so she buys Wind Drift Cologne, and Timberline Cologne, then grins at us, "Because some

BASSETT BEDDING   Is Gene Shalit, the TV film reviewer, inviting housewives to pat the bed next to him? (*opposite*)
THERMOS   For the tiniest of straplines, she uses the Even-Up Tanning Blanket. (*above*)

like it cool, and some like it hot." Subtle they're not, any more than the After Six Formals commercial showing a couple kissing passionately for fourteen seconds; just in time we pull back slowly to see that we are at a wedding, and they are now man and wife. They go on kissing while the announcer says, "After Six is delighted to sponsor . . . some of the most beautiful moments of your life." No censorship problems here, because the final scene is surrounded by a wedding band.

Most ads don't offer us such unflinching titillation; instead, they're more like glances—a girl scampers past the camera, holding the strings of her bikini top behind her back. Her voice whispers on the sound track: "What do you do when a string breaks?" Her back is on screen for three seconds, but her bikini top does look like it may fall off, which is enough to keep people watching while the announcer tells them that when you feel anxious and sweaty, you need Soft and Dry. We witness again the curious attraction-and-censorship routine: the ad writer connects deodorant with nervous sweating, and nervousness with exposure, possibly with exhibitionism, and then, in the spot, *almost* reveals this girl's nipples, but saves public decency by one broken thread.

"I don't wear panties any more," whispers one model, suggesting that she may be ready for instant liaison. But cleanliness prevails! That is *not* why she doesn't wear panties. "It's because under all my dresses, under all my thin knits, under all my slightly tight pants, I wear Underalls." We get to see her ass wiggling in each outfit as she goes on to challenge the viewer to look very closely: "So there's never a panty line or a bump or a bulge to show through your clothes." With that presentation, no man is going to think about aesthetics or comfort when he watches this commercial, and no woman is, either. But the ad writer saves us from feeling guilty about it by saying, in effect—no, no, Underalls are just to make clothes look better.

I like competing

Then if I win,

I like the way it smells on men. And I like the kind of men who wear it. I find them to be challenging. When it comes to the battle of the sexes, I don't like pushovers.

against men.

But only when they

don't patronize me.

it's really exciting.

You know what else I find exciting?
Men who wear English Leather
Cologne.

I guess that's why all my men wear
English Leather, or they wear nothing
at all.

ENGLISH LEATHER Voted sexiest spot on the air
by numerous men, this sweaty drama comes on breathing hard.

(MUSIC) ANNOUNCER: Introducing Smitty, the spirited, sexy new fragrance by Coty.

When you're stayin' out late . . . and you're feelin' just great . . .

All the world's gonna know . . . Smitty did it.

Most such semi-obscene commercials aim at women. Some are midday porn. Lifebuoy soap, for instance, sponsors hairy-chested guys getting out of their workshirts, staring soulfully into the camera, inviting us into the shower with them, to get all lathered up. And Mennen's Speed Stick features a muscular outdoor man, naked from the waist up, with his arms lifted in the air. He turns to us and says, "I got held up every morning. . . ." He turns, and we see that he has a taut belly and a hairy chest. We move in on his blue eyes as he completes his sentence (if anyone is still listening): ". . . waiting for my roll-on antiperspirant to dry."

Another kind of ad directed at women's erotic subconscious relies on fear rather than sex as a stimulant. This anxiety outsells chest shots, to judge from the number of commercials aimed at the woman who is desperate to get a man. This is an old theme (we've heard it in hundreds of mouthwash and deodorant commercials), but there are always new variations; "Monday I wore a turtle, and Mike said, 'What eyes!' Tueday I wore jodhpurs, and Mike said, 'What lips.' Wednesday I wore a babushka, and Mike said . . . 'What is this? Are you bald?' " She did not dare show him her dull, flat, dirty hair. But then she found Prell Concentrate. And, because her hair was so fluffy on Thursday, Mike asked her out again for Friday.

Sponsors now claim their products help women "do it." Coty, for instance, makes Smitty, and they bill it as the spirited and sexy new fragrance. We see a girl with fluffy hair dancing in a disco; a man kisses her neck while she laughs; in the next shot her hair is flying as she swoops down; then she bumps her rear toward him; swings with him; swoops away; laughs; moves in for a kiss, and, laughing, accepts his buss on her jugular. The lead singer in the band sings, "Well, it just goes to show . . . when you're feeling that glow . . . all the world's gonna know . . . Smitty did it." The chorus chimes in, "Smitty did it."

As *Newsweek* commented in 1968, when the sexy sell had just come in, "TV commercials have always used pretty girls to make a pitch. But while their sex was feminine, their sell was largely neuter. For one thing, ad men feared that overly sexy models would alienate women viewers, who do most of the family buying. For another, they suspected that male viewers ogling a sultry girl would forget the product. Consequently, top commercial spokeswomen like Betty Furness tended to display about as much sex appeal as the refrigerators they ballyhooed."

Even today, whether the ads are sultry or cool, they are still mainly tissues of suggestion rather than frontal display. And every suggestion turns out to be a disappointment. If you're aroused, the sex object of your choice tries to sell you something. If you think that for once this commercial is going to get past a happy, laughing kiss on the run, you're in for a letdown.

That's what happens when a beautiful sixteen-year-old girl whispers in one spot that she has just met a cute boy, but he has pimples. So, she reports, she said to him, "Why don't you come over to my pad?" Maybe she's heard that pimples come from too much chastity. *Variety*'s critic, Carroll Carroll, blathers that this is "Another plug for the new sleep-around way of growing up." But the girl hasn't invited the boy up to her bedroom. She's offering him a medicated face wipe called Stridex. How's that for a cold shower?

Alas, there is not enough real sex in commercials. And audiences settle for suggestions. Who knows what they do with those hints, those three-second glimpses, inside their unconscious minds? Clearly, enough fantasizing goes on to make hundreds of thousands of viewers reach for the product associated with sex on the very next day. But what about the constant disappointment, the perpetual stopping before climax, this foreplay without orgasm? With commercials like these, we experience an ongoing cycle of arousal but deprivation. Perhaps that satisfies the other part of our mind—the more cautious, the more critical, the more Puritan fraction—our superego.

Censorship pays. It keeps the veils on—so instead of showing the real thing, these commercials provide a unique American striptease, rich in promise but overdressed in moral bunkum.

SMITTY, BY COTY The chorus exults, "Smitty did it, Smitty did it." Evidently the perfume gave her hair those strong back-lights, the hectic energy for dancing, and the final kiss. (*opposite*)
FRUIT OF THE LOOM They're not selling apples or legs, though both are open to the halfway mark: can't you see she's wearing panty hose? (*right*)

ANNOUNCER: You know this famous Fruit of the Loom symbol.

But did you know you can buy beautiful . . .

Fruit of the Loom pantyhose for under a dollar a pair? Why pay more?

emotional

We are sitting in a grimy diner. A middle-aged man with three days' stubble on his chin leans over the Formica counter. Out of the air a woman's voice says, "Robert Lent, eat your soup."

He looks up. "Is that you, Ma?"

She coos, "Poor baby, tired, lonely, and hungry, and all you're having to eat is a cheeseburger? Remember how good Campbell's tomato soup always made you feel, how warm and soothing it was?"

"Oh yeah," he says, lost in memories.

"So why not have a big steaming bowl of it right now? You'll feel better."

"Oh yes," he says, near swooning.

We see a shot of the product, and her attention turns to us. "America, eat your Campbell's soup; it'll make you feel better."

Mom sells. Nostalgia for home, memories of childhood, a kid's longing for love from Mom and Grandma, these outsell the urge for sex and the itch for violence. Even fear, which grimaces in so many spots pushing deodorants, masks a kid's desperate cry for attention and affection from Mom. To judge from commercials, it is Mom who best cajoles, argues, charms, and scares us into buying. And Mom doesn't offer us rational arguments; she persuades us by appealing to our most childish impulses.

In the mythic world of commercials, the family represents paradise. A teary mist often drifts over scenes in which the family gathers around the huge table filled with food; light glows around Mom, Dad, and Grandpa; we look up at them from a kid's eye level; we hear sentimental music keening in the background, and the text emphasizes loss. How long ago! How perfect it was! If only we could get back to that bliss, we are encouraged to imagine, then we could be a bubbly baby again; Mom would feed us till we burped; Dad would care; Grandma and Grandpa would play with us again.

In commercials you can go home again. And even in spots that do not explicitly take us back to the good old days, we find Mom, the ultimate authority, playing on our emotions. Mom tucks us in with the right brand of sheets, the right medicine, the right food; she takes care of us by buying right. And sometimes she weeps for the days when we were babies and the family was a living unit, not just a memory or dream. She makes us feel nostalgic and snuffly. And when we don't buy what she recommends, she yells at us or, more subtly, sobs some more, to make us feel guilty, too. With luck, she makes us literally cry for a product.

"Is it good sales practice to make people cry?" asks Ron Hoff, a top writer at Foote Cone & Belding. "My answer to that is, man, I'd like to move them emotionally, whether it's laughter or tears or whatever it generates; it's got to stick in your mind if you respond emotionally to a commercial."

What emotions sell best? Which emotions are people willing to pay for—by buying the product—to recall the commercial and thereby resuscitate that cherished feeling? At first people are aware of tender moments—they long to feel love and comfort. They dream of togetherness—in the family, on the block, in the larger political community. But many people remember undercurrents of guilt, fear, rage, and depression running through years of childhood: and evidently one way for these people to go "home" is to reexperience these emotions, particularly in scenes showing Mom and the family. So in commercials Mom may smile, but she also jabs her finger at us, yelling and threatening. Most frightening of all, she may collapse in front of us, helpless, but not too helpless to point out that we could cheer her up by buying something for her —flowers, a phone call, even a card.

Some obvious emotionalism in commercials seems deliberate—the result of an adman's sly guesses about our unconscious. But sometimes things go wrong and the adman thinks he is ap-

Reproduced with the permission of PepsiCo, Inc. "Pepsi" and "Pepsi-Cola" are registered trademarks of PepsiCo, Inc.

pealing to one emotion while unconsciously he is actually arousing another. If the adman does not understand his own emotional investment in the commercial, the scene may backfire in his face. Thus commercials do not create these moods, these myths; they reflect them, and they try to capitalize on them. Commercials simply underline our society's unconscious mental life, tears and all.

One commercial that made thousands of hardened ad people cry in award ceremonies around the world starts outside a one-family suburban house with Mom calling, "Hey, someone tell Grandma the movers are here." We cut to the attic. A little boy asks Grandma: "Grandma, how come you have to move from your house?" We see trunks, boxes, old clothes. Grandma answers, "Because it's too big; I don't need all this room now that everybody's got their own home." She seems tough, brave almost, but falls off toward the end, near tears.

The boy is kind: "Can we come visit you in your new apartment?"

"I certainly hope so," says Grandma. "Oh, look . . . this is very special. These are my cards." She has found a dusty hatbox. "These are birthday cards, get-well cards, and all the lovely cards people have sent me since I was as young as you are." She breathes a bit wheezily between each packet of cards. "You remember this one, it's the one you sent me last spring when I was in the hospital." She sounds warm and misty, then gruff and grown-up; the actress wobbles near sobs, then recovers and talks like a parent. She recalls her first anniversary. The kid finds a big hat, and Grandma reaches for it, trying it on again.

Mom bursts into the attic now, saying, "Mother, Mother, the movers are here. We've got to get going. You have everything you want? The movers can pack the rest."

Mom exits, leaving Grandma to her memories. She looks in the mirror, sniffs, then recovers and laughs. As she leads the boy downstairs, the announcer comes in: "Greeting cards: they can keep a lifetime of memories safe and secure. Hallmark: when you care enough to send the very best."

I've seen that three times and cried every time. Why? She's brave, she's pitiful; and I used to save my letters, my toys, anything that would

PEPSI Good times with Grandma culminate with a romp with her new pups. Then she serves Pepsi.

help me remember the good old days, so I know the impulse, and this is the very scene I was preparing for when I crated up every postcard I ever got. Someday *I* would be old and sad, and, yes, these cards would make me realize once upon a time I was loved.

Hallmark knew that when they proposed this commercial. And yet the writing was not simply a calculated attempt to trade on sentiment. Ron Hoff, who worked on it, was recalling his own family, his own mother. "There were a lot of things that went into that commercial. One was a feeling I had that all middle-aged people feel guilty about their parents, particularly when their parents reach their seventies and eighties. You really feel you're not spending enough time with them. Then, the single act of the parent moving from the home where the family has grown up into a smaller home, which is what the older people always do, is probably the most dramatic and significant sign of the mortality of the whole family. The family is changing. The mother is going to die. Moving away from the house where you grew up, boy, that's a misty experience. It's the end of childhood. And the mother has to move away because we grew up. It's gotta be a profoundly moving experience if you've got a sense of family, as I think most Americans do.

"But that was also probably the most competitive commercial that Hallmark ever did. Hallmark's competition isn't American Greeting Cards. Hallmark's competition is the telephone and flowers. You either send a card or you call or you wire Mother flowers. And a telephone call is a very ephemeral thing: you make it, and it disappears; flowers are perishable. But here is a lady going back fifteen or twenty years, showing that cards, while not

MOTHER: We're here.
SON: Grandpa's house?

For a vacation, or a visit

Stretching your dollar

AMERICAN AIRLINES The whole family gets into this brief but emotional drama. There are tears on each face, and a comforting hug at the end.

FATHER: Almost . . . let's go.

ANNOUNCER: No matter where you fly on American Airlines,

no one offers a lower fare.

to someone you love . . .

. . . far away.

(MUSIC RISES)

is one of the things we do best.

We're American Airlines.

We're American Airlines.
Doing what we do best.

Call us or your Travel Agent.

CHORUS SINGS: We're American Airlines.
Doing what we do best.

(SOUND OF STORM)
FATHER: It's crazy to let them go
out on a night like this.

MOTHER: But she's waited
months for tonight.

(DOORBELL RINGS)
DAUGHTER: Mom, is that Jeff?

MOTHER: Hello, Jeff.
JEFF: Mrs. Stewart. Mr. Stewart.
FATHER: Jeff.

JEFF: Hi.

FATHER: Jeff, do me a favor, will
you? Take my Volvo.

ANNOUNCER: Over the years,
safety has been an obsession
with Volvo.

Because of all the things that go
into a Volvo,

the ones we've always valued
most . . . are people.
MOTHER: Be careful.

eternal, certainly last longer than a phone call."

The Bell Telephone System fights that claim with emotional fire of its own. In one of their commercials a woman with a foreign accent talks over a song, of which we only hear the refrain ("Memories light the corners of my mind"). She says, "What remains vivid in my memory is my husband with a bunch of suitcases, my little child on my hands, and all of us being pushed up this staircase, and I remember all of us looking back and seeing my mother and father crying and sort of blowing their noses with their handkerchiefs." The announcer suggests she call them. We see two simple peasants sitting by a whitewashed wall. The phone rings. They answer it, overwhelmed by the miracle of overseas telephonic connection. They are back together again.

Home—to judge only from commercials—is a powerful totem to Americans. Pan Am's most effective advertising doesn't urge you to travel to exotic places, but to go "home." "In America there are millions of Italians who have never seen Italy." We see Italo-Americans, then Rome. "And Poles who have never seen Poland and Japanese who have never seen Japan and millions of Germans who have never seen Germany. Not to mention the Scandinavians who have never seen Scandinavia, and the Latins, English, and Africans who have never seen those places, and that is kind of a shame." And Allegheny Airlines reminds us, "We were born in America's hometowns. . . . And we still take that real hometown feeling along with us." And American Airlines shows a little boy and his parents walking out of a plane. The grandparents see them. Dad shows the kid where they are. Grandma half smiles, half cries. Granddad's mouth turns down. Mom beams through her tears. The kid starts running. Granddad bends down. The kid hugs him. CHORUS: "We're American Airlines, doing what we do best." Right out of Norman Rockwell.

VOLVO A funny/sad spot in which Dad protects his daughter by letting Jeff take his Volvo on a rainy night.

Of course, you could be content with just photographs. A woman's voice says, "Good morning, yesterday. You wake up and time has slipped away." She's wandering around a house in which bare floors and boxes tell us it's moving day. She has gray hair. She looks at a broken mirror. "Suddenly it's hard to find the memories you left behind . . . the good times and the bad you've seen." We see her, much younger, bringing in a birthday cake; the kids blow out the candles; we see the son bringing out the dog; we see the kids grown up, graduating, married, and now the two old parents are out in front at the gate, looking back at the house, chock full of Kodak memories. As the moving van pulls up, they brush back their tears and kiss.

Such bittersweet nostalgia for home and family seems to be something we enjoy. The FTC claims that the purpose of advertising is to provide the consumer with enough information to make a rational decision in the marketplace. But one adman argues that the best commercials have to go "beyond information." Walter Taplin, author of a textbook on advertising, says, "Anyone who wishes to tell anyone about goods and services which may help him to spend his life in a fuller or more pleasant manner automatically goes far beyond the sphere of information. He is dealing with vague wants, unformed desires, wants which have not become conscious, and with an infinite field of alternatives, not one of which is essential. It is a sphere in which human beings become more than calculating machines or mere brutes concerned with food and shelter. The world of weights and measures s left behind. What is the good of providing facts about wine to a man who has never tasted it? The liter measure, alcoholic content, country of origin, and price mean little to him. Still less do the refinements of year, area, vineyard, and character. Even when he has tasted it, he may not like it. In fact, most of the things we want are not material but mental. We want states of mind. The advertiser, beginning with a material object which is to be sold, suggests the states of mind which may be achieved by the purchaser." Perhaps that is what Inglenook had in mind when they created their ad in which a daughter remembers graduating from medical school. She came home, Dad got the Inglenook wine out of the linen closet to celebrate and they all lifted their glasses: "To my daughter, the doctor." It's a child's dream: after hard work, to be accepted by Mom and Dad, to be celebrated by them. In this way Inglenook is made to seem like a gold star.

Parental approval—or disapproval—sells margarine, too, as Joe Brown found out when he was working for Cunningham & Walsh on the Chiffon Margarine account. He was looking for an authority figure to testify that Chiffon tasted just like butter. "Rather than some cooking authority, which some of the competitors were using, we chose Mother Nature. Who could know more what real butter should taste like? And almost immediately the brand sales took off. These commercials have scored well above the average on recall. One scored near the upper three percent of all commercials ever tested."

So actress Dena Dietrich gets dressed up in a white gown, with a crown of daisies, and when children offer her Chiffon, she says it's butter,

MAN SINGING: There's nothing like the face

of a kid eating a Hershey bar.

and they laugh, saying, "No, it's not." Then, because "It's not nice to fool Mother Nature," she unleashes some natural disaster—lightning over Grand Canyon, snow in a redwood forest, simple rain on kids in a picnic area. The kids never get hurt, but the explosion—and complete change in the weather—always delights audiences.

People seem actually to like remembering Mom getting angry. It makes us all feel like kids again, lying low together until Mom's fury —at unwashed dishes, unbrushed teeth—subsides. In one toothpaste commercial a mother blows up about "The excuses I got when they had to brush their teeth!" Then, she tells us, she switched to Aim. And now the kids rush in and brush—"willingly, and maybe longer." The same problem was presented more dramatically in this Gleem commercial: Mom comes into the bathroom, gets out the Gleem, spreads it on the toothbrush, and hides herself behind the door. Her son comes in. She lunges at him, toothbrush in hand. He flees, knocking over the laundry. She falls flat. He leaps over her and runs out into the hall and downstairs. She slides down the bannister behind him and runs into the piano. He loses sight of her and decides to hide in the bathroom. When he closes the door, there she is. She forces the Gleem-covered toothbrush into his mouth. He smiles. He begins to brush voluntarily while the announcer nods, "We found that no matter what kind of toothpaste you use, it won't fight cavities unless your kid brushes with it. And nothing makes a kid want to brush more than a toothpaste that tastes good." Except maybe a psychotic mother.

Such confrontations are mainly the exception, not the rule, and affectionate tolerance patches up any possible conflict between Mom and the Kid. In one cough medicine commercial a teen-aged boy says, "Whenever I have a bad cold my mother spoils me." We cut to a view of her sitting in the back room, knitting. "Look at all these medicines!" the boy exclaims. Unnecessary, we understand, because "All I really do is get Nyquil, the nighttime cold medicine." Suddenly Mom appears and hovers over him. "Got everything you need, son?" she asks tenderly. We know he does, despite her having bought all those useless competitors of Nyquil; we also know he'll ignore them in favor of Nyquil. But at least she cares, right? He turns to us and confides, "She's terrific."

HERSHEY Trading on memories of getting candy from Dad, these spots reassure parents that their child will beam if they give him a Hershey bar.

Any attack on Mom—one of the central figures in American mythology—has to be apologized for right away. Most admen play it safe, and just praise Mom and her wonderful family. And Mom's usually the star, particularly when she is taking care of you. "I remember when I had my first baby, a beautiful experience for a woman, and the joy of knowing my baby was healthy," says a mother who uses Pampers, and, naturally, she concludes, "A baby is a gift people give each other." And when enough babies come (2.6, for example), you reach that idyllic state, a family. The Jones family—a real family actually—makes and advertises Jones Dairy Farm pork sausage, and we see the whole family sitting around the breakfast table while Uncle Ed talks about honest-to-goodness ingredients. The feeling: down-home farm folk, eating together, the way a family should. Other members of the ideal family include Dad, who plays with you and gives you Life Savers, or chocolate bars while a singer proclaims, "There's nothing like the face of a kid eating a Hershey bar. A face as happy as can be." But Dad can be eliminated. The key image is that of Mom and the kids, as in the Allstate ad, in which Dad tells us that they have bought insurance. Mom hugs the two kids, and Dad takes their picture, saying, "So this family will always be in good hands . . . even if I'm not in the picture." The picture is, of course, Mom, dead center, being kissed by one son and one daughter.

Even when Mother plays second fiddle to her daughter, she sells products. In one Johnson & Johnson spot we see a mother sitting in front of a mirror while her daughter scurries around getting ready for her wedding. The mother finds Johnson & Johnson baby powder on the dressing table: we see her remember when her daughter was just a baby. She begins to cry. The daughter comforts her. Says the pseudonymous Carl Wrighter, "This is one of the most touching commercials around. It's real, identifiable, and rings true. But what is it saying? Logically, nothing. Just that a lot of mothers have used the stuff for a long time. But emotionally, it's a grabber. Because that mother is every mother, and her tears are tears of joy, tinged with just a little heartbreak at losing her daughter... The point is, Mother is out there merchandising, with happiness, tears, and love."

Some pitches make us feel like concerned parents. In 1964 Tony Schwartz invented an anti-Goldwater spot for Lyndon Johnson: it showed a little girl picking daisies, followed by a film of a nuclear bomb exploding and President Johnson's voice pleading: Either we must love one another or die. The appeal was in the little girl; the message—a vote for Goldwater is a vote against innocent children. Schwartz laughs at ads that try to reason with a customer or aim to make a consumer recall certain words the announcer spoke. Smart ads evoke emotions already in the consumer's mind and urge the consumer to act on those feelings. Schwartz says, "When I was asked by the American Cancer Society back in the Sixties to create a TV spot that would encourage people to give up smoking, I did not ask, 'What can I say to convince people to stop smoking?' Rather, I attempted to evoke feelings based on a listener viewer's experience that might lead to the desired change in behavior, given the likely context in which my stimuli would be seen and heard. The spot I designed shows two children dressing up in their parents' clothes. At the end, a voice-over announcer says very calmly, 'Children love to imitate their parents—children learn by imitating their parents. Do you smoke cigarettes?' The American Cancer Society said it was the most successful spot they ever ran, and they subsequently used the theme in other ads. The anti-smoking *message* was not in the words or visual of the commercial, but in the feelings evoked by the commercial stimuli."

Politicians use these appeals to emotion constantly, perhaps because they're running for the post of Dad. On TV they must stop talking as if they were addressing a crowded hall—after all, TV is an intimate medium, and the set is within conversational distance. For a politician, credibility means intimacy, according to numerous experts—casualness, spontaneity, lots of eye contact, ineffable warmth, in brief, the contact we seek from a father. "Of course, the issues are important," intones Daniel Yankelovich. "But personality is more critical. Credibility is what the voter is looking for." Richard Nixon's shifty eyes and unshaven jowl lost him votes in 1960 when compared to John Kennedy's ease, flexibility, and occasional direct appeals to the audience. When candidates Nixon and Kennedy were asked what they would do about Harry Truman swearing in public, Nixon frowned and declaimed; Kennedy laughed—and won. Jimmy Carter's sweater, put on for his first carefully arranged fireside chat on energy, was a calculated piece of iconography: when Dad seems friendly, relaxed, willing to suffer along with us—as Carter was supposed to appear—we vote for him; when, like Nixon, he calls us all children and boasts about being tough, we may vote for him, but we also tend to recall childhood resentment at Dad. Nixon's support melted away, in part, because he won it with commercials that aroused our fear rather than our friendliness.

Fear and its transcendence—trust, sympathy, friendliness—are almost as important emotional selling points as Home and Mother. The lump in your throat tells you so when, on your TV screen, you watch a young girl say, "I'm going blind. The disease I have, something called Retinitis Pigmentosa, is taking my sight away. Little by little." The screen dims, goes black. This is frightening. What can be done? We think. Thank goodness ITT has a device that can help. We see the girl through the device; she is green but clear. She holds up the device in front of her. "To you, this may seem ugly. To me, it's beautiful." And indeed, the story is beautiful.

Fear is also transcended, this time by friendliness, in a Della Femina spot for ABC Eye-witness News. Here we see the Eyewitness News Team in the entrance to what seems to be a building in East Harlem. A man is saying to them, "Come on, I guarantee everyone a good time." Dubious, the group stands looking up some shabby stairs, listening to the bad Latin music above. They go up into the second-floor Puerto Rican social club. Some people are dancing at the far side of the room, but they stop when the Team enters. There is silence. A pause. Everyone is frozen. This could be a bad moment. But the anonymous guide shouts, "My good friends, I'd like you to meet my good friends Melba, Roger, Tex, Frank, Phil, and Jim." There is another pause. Then a fat Latin woman waves. "Hello, Roger Grimsby." She crosses to him and sweeps him up to dance. Soon they are all dancing together. Ah, humanity!

The same impulse lies behind another commercial by the Della Femina crew which shows a mother and father sweating out a Little League game in the stands; they are Japanese, and the announcer comments, "People are pretty much the same all over when it comes to taking pictures, except for the film they use." The umpire calls their son out. The kid pouts. Pop goes to yell at the ump. Mom consoles the kid. We pull back slowly as the announcer plugs Fuji film: "Try it on your favorite baseball player. Japanese color is here." This visual plug for universal brotherhood comes from the same man who once suggested selling Panasonic TV sets with the line: "From the wonderful folks who brought you Pearl Harbor."

Georgia-Pacific shows us a barn-raising, a community effort. "Friends come from miles around to help . . ." says the announcer, and the fiddle goes *mm hhmmm* as the men start putting up the frame, the logs, the plywood, all with the large logo, GP. "But we're more than just timber." We see different people hoisting up even more products from Georgia-Pacific: gypsum board, plastic pipe, asphalt tiles. Then the dinner bell rings, and we see the whole town gather around the long table. After dinner the good farm folk line up and lead a cow into the barn as everyone pats it. "We even provide part of the feed that will make the cattle feel at home in

ITT   It looks real, but it's a dummy, built by ITT to imitate a real person undergoing heart surgery at the University of Miami Medical School; as we watch students cut the mannequin open, the sound track of the heartbeat rises in crescendo.

their new home." The populist romanticism of such a spot overtly encourages people to work with each other, and (the advertiser hopes) makes the audience identify Georgia-Pacific with those solid, down-home values.

The dizzy ideal of such togetherness is the intended effect of Coca-Cola's whirlwind tour of the world: "I'd like to teach the world to sing in perfect harmony." Everyone around the world is smiling, joining hands, coming together. It's all a little too perfect, but for that lump-in-the-throat feeling it can't compete with the ad Mc-Donald's ran just before the 1976 Olympic Games. It showed a fourteen-year-old in a yel-

low jacket running with his dog up a hill, then over a bridge. His feet are pounding, and we hear him mutter, "I'm gonna win that medal." We see a truck with two country fellers in it; they say, "There goes Alvin." The driver honks: "Hi, Alvin." Small-town togetherness. Alvin keeps on running. Two old geezers lounge on a porch. "That boy sure likes to run," says one. The other agrees. "He sure does." They know him, too. He must be part of the community. Now the chorus comes in softly. "You, you're the one." As Alvin passes the sheep, we begin to see fast shots of the Olympic races intercut between shots of Alvin running. In slow motion

ANNOUNCER: When you consider that heart disease is the nation's number one killer, you can see where Harvey has quite a future.

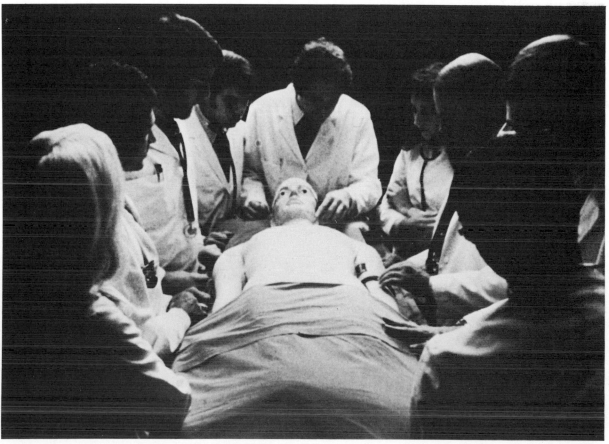

he leaps a stream. In slow motion a hurdler clears the last obstacle to victory on the Olympic track. Applause soars at the Olympic stadium. Alvin surges through his own fence at the same time that the American star bursts the tape. Alvin stands up proudly, his imagination full of victory. The crowd goes wild; the chorus peaks; the announcer says, "On the occasion of the 1976 Olympic Games, McDonald's salutes the determination and persistence of America's youth." So there you have it all: the feeling of community, the pride in our representative, the national glory of winning the Olympics, the massed voices in chorus and applause, and the ambition of youth.

That's emotionalism, all right. And it may sell hamburgers. But it also lights an Olympic flame in young minds.

So the unconscious, restless for Mom, frightened, lustful, cruel, may also yearn for union with humanity as a larger family. And since our unconscious cannot tell the difference between dream and reality, it mistakes buying a product for being fed, washed, praised, hugged, or protected. Buying a product or a candidate, then, becomes a way to regain the fantasy satisfactions once more, no matter what the real cost.

Perhaps that is the role of faith in a consumer society. But who knows which family feelings will work best for a particular product? Would guilt sell Xerox, for instance? Would fear? What emotions can I evoke to sell my product? sponsors ask. For an answer, many corporations turn to motivational research. This technique, and the term, come from a firm run by Dr. Ernest Dichter, one of the early personifications of what Vance Packard, in 1957, called *The Hidden Persuaders*. Dr. Dichter (the name means *poet* in German) counsels corporations on the Freudian meanings of their products. During the Fifties the California Prune Advisory Board came to him to find out why so few people were buying prunes; Dr. Dichter sent his workers out

BLUE CROSS/BLUE SHIELD OF GREATER NEW YORK This scary spot warns us that "People are getting careless. Four out of ten preschool children in this country are not immunized against polio. Some may get caught. Don't let it happen to your kids."

ANNOUNCER: Polio isn't dead.

It's just sleeping . . . and waiting.

Because if children don't get immunized against polio—it comes back.

to give word association tests. What they found was that prunes were associated with old maids, old prune faces, those dried-up old prunes. Prunes were forced on children, so they were as yucky as anything else that is just "good for you." Prunes were black, like witches, like death. Prunes gave you the runs. Dr. Dichter felt that "The taste story had become lost." He suggested a more dynamic image: "Call it the new wonder fruit." Bright colors should be used for advertising and packaging; kids and pretty girls should be shown eating prunes. The new slogan became, "Get that top-of-the-world feeling." Thanks to their new image as a merry-go-round of health and sociability, prunes started up on the sales charts, and even in years when most crops were dropping in price and profit, the prune kept expanding its market.

Asked for similar help for tea, Dr. Dichter found that Americans thought of tea as "something for when you're sick." Plus Chinese drank that stuff. And old ladies. And those English sissies. Dr. Dichter suggested that when schoolteachers tell their students about the Boston Tea Party they remind the kids that Americans had dumped tea in Boston Harbor because they were mad about tea—for it, not against it. But tea needed a macho image to overcome the idea that it might be "weak" or effeminate. Use bright red, he suggested. Talk tough. The Tea Council

slogan became, "Make it hefty, hot, and hearty." Sales went up from thirteen to twenty-five percent, depending on the area.

Dr. Dichter is working on soap now. His research convinces him that Americans take baths these days for fun. "Americans are taking baths and showers together often to feel a sense of absolution from sex." They are washing away the guilt of being naked together, he thinks. So he's designing a soap that can be passed back and forth between consenting partners, even in a slippery shower. The palm is essential to Dichter's theorizing. "It helps to look at it as zoology—what do humans have in common with apes? For example, the desire to grasp."

In probing people's feelings for profit, Dr. Dichter has come up with an interesting model of the best commercial: it should invite the audience to participate; it should offer to boost their egos; it should work on a nonverbal level; it should condense a great many messages into one scene; it should include something that will trigger action; it should rehearse the actual purchase; and, most important, it should establish a definite emotional mood.

Some agencies carry out their own version of motivational research by means of something they call focus groups. Here, a savvy therapist-cum-interviewer hired by the ad agency talks around a table with a group of so-called average consumers, trying to find out their real feelings about the product, the way they use it, the secret resentments they have, their desires, their conflicts. Sometimes the manufacturer sits behind a smoked-glass partition listening, and occasionally he doesn't hear what he wants. One exec got so furious at the answers one woman gave to the interviewer that he broke into the room and yelled at her, "You're so dumb you don't deserve a good mouthwash."

Intuitive guesses, hunches, reasonable guestimates do come out of this kind of research. Sometimes these are backed up by more scientific surveys, complete with double-blinds, significance curves, and sociological jargon. Agencies hire outside management consultant teams to perform the legwork on 75 percent of these surveys, but design the questionnaires and proof the statistics themselves.

But motivational research fails as often as it succeeds in finding the emotional trigger that touches off the impulse to buy. Vance Packard convinced millions that ad execs do know what they are doing. In a staff report to the Federal Trade Commission, Professors John Howard and James Hulbert point out that this is not true. At the moment, they say, "Motivational research possesses no special proclivity for unconsciously or unfairly influencing the consumer; it is merely another tool of research, no less fallible, and possibly more fallible than other methods." They admit that even after months of hearings, "The Commissioners [of the FTC] did not learn what they had hoped to learn: what kinds of ads have what kinds of effects on purchasing behavior. They did learn, contrary to what they thought, that advertisers do not typically know how to reach a given, specialized, relevant audience with any degree of accuracy."

So ad writers still have to rely on their own instinct, and that instinct may be skewed by emotion: the impulses that inspire the ads become the feelings that the ads arouse. Some ad-

men write commercials in which the characters simply dance out the activity that the sponsor dreams of after a three-hour lunch—customers scream delight at seeing the product, throw down wads of money to buy another case, push the product on friends. Such commercials seem to treat the audience as so many puppets.

Part of the problem is that for all the probes of consumers, admen do not always examine their own impulses. In the day-to-day pressure of deadlines and profit statements, some ad people may come to see the client as an angry and unfriendly father, well worth frustrating; and the stubborn consumer, who just will not buy the product, may end up being pushed around the way a younger sibling gets sneered at by the older ones. The result: commercials that unconsciously attack the audience and therefore end up turning the audience against the product.

In one chewing gum commercial, for instance, we see people staggering around trying to talk, but not being able to, because of huge labels over their mouths. The pieces of paper say, "Don't open 'til Beechnut." Now this campaign must have some rationale behind it: there must have been the usual big meeting with Beechnut, and after much highfalutin discussion, this commercial emerged. But what everyone at that meeting, agency and sponsor alike, forgot was that we identify with these people: we don't like having paper over our mouths. This may fulfill the fantasies of some Beechnut executives, but we still do not want to be gagged, and we tend to hate anyone who wants to shut us up.

Unconscious rage at the consumer shows up in snide and vicious razzing of innocent characters like us. Continental Airlines sends out a flying squad of stewardesses to pursue an innocent man coming into an airport; he has chosen to fly some other airline, not Continental, and they follow him like children mocking a schoolmate. "You'll miss our movie show," they taunt. They make such an ugly scene, surrounding him and teasing him, that he finally breaks down and says, "Boohoo."

Another commercial starts off with a sneering voice-over that says, "This is Harry beside his car. Harry's also beside himself because the top of his car looks like the bottom. And his dashboard's no spring chicken, either. But Harry's in for a little surprise." A new product called Son of a Gun pops up. Harry looks at it, but he has been deprived of a sound track so that this announcer can call the shots. "Put some on the top, Harry. Rub it around a little. That's it. Now what'd ya say? Right. Son of a Gun. Try it on the dashboard." Now Harry gets run through a minor Olympics cleaning the door panels, the weather strips, the tires, the golf bags in the back. Then his wife appears, grabs the can of Son of a Gun and, at the voice-over's orders, goes into the house and cleans the refrigerator, picture frames, handbags, suitcases, shoes, boots, the hi-fi, two chairs, and the vinyl upholstery on a sofa. The fast cuts and the insistent control of sound by the announcer make this couple seem like speechless slaves, bullied into action by the sponsor, STP. Not very friendly.

Probably no one at the ad agency thought that we might feel pushed around by this announcer. Such feelings, I am sure, got submerged under much talk about how many product advantages were being shown, and how often the brand name was being repeated. But if admen can be so unconscious of the emotions they themselves experience, they may be passing along those emotions to us.

And the dominant emotion in many ad offices is fear. "Make no mistake, fear of the new grips agencies as much as it does clients—sometimes even more," says Alvin Hampel, executive president of Benton & Bowles. "Interestingly, it's not so much fear of the idea itself but fear of looking silly to the client." And James Jordan, head of Batten Barton Durstine & Osborn, says, "Almost nobody writes in a rage these days. Many people write in a cold sweat. They write out of fear. Fear of their bosses, fear of their clients, fear of the lawyers, fear of research and development, fear of the networks, fear of the Feds, fear of Burke, A.S.I. [two companies that test audience response to commercials]." Under this fear lies an animal rage at the people who terrify the copywriter most: his boss, his client, then his audience. When the ad writer notices these feelings in himself, though, he seems able to reassert the capitalist faith that if we buy something, Mom and Dad will be OK, no matter who wants to mug them—or us.

Naturally, such fear—and faith—sometimes creeps into commercials, no matter what they sell. Arco takes us around the dark city in the cab of a street sweeper. The driver says, "I used to go by this alley that was so badly lit, there were two or three muggings a week." There is a clang. The cop on the beat spins around with his flashlight. It is just a dog scavenging. "So I wrote the Mayor. It took a while. But one night there it was. My street lamp. Shining like the sun." An elderly couple get off a bus and look shakily at a teenager. The teenager comes up to them threateningly, but sees the light and gives up. Arco has saved Mom and Dad.

Other spots scare us with symptoms. Three men who talk strangely tell us they all had cancer. They are using voice boxes to speak. Do not smoke, they tell us: or else. Or there is the spot for polio. "Polio isn't dead. It's just sleeping . . . and waiting." We pan across a room full of iron lungs. "People are getting careless," says Blue Cross/Blue Shield. Like Mom warning us about relatives who died from stepping on a rusty nail, the ad scares, yet promises a way out, if we just subscribe.

Having established a world of fear, the ad-maker can introduce the product as combined parent and genie. The parents' power resembles that of God. They set up Eden, then drove us out. They could still feed us the milk of paradise, if we would just lift our wallet in their direction. Mom makes us feel guilt, fear, and rage. By watching these spots, and by buying the products, we can quiet unhappy feelings and stay in touch with our memories of a frightening, frustrating, only occasionally tender life at home. In this commercial myth, products are like mother's milk—they relieve tense bellies, soothe fevered heads, ease our anger, allay our fears. And at the same time, the products keep us in a child's role—dependent and clamoring for more.

The childlike awe at the corporate Mom and her amazing "gifts" encourages a capitalist faith, then—in gadgets, in whatever money can buy, in team play, and in individual success. Like babies at the teat, we hate to give up our push-button blessings.

Xerox, for example, plays God for Brother Benedict, who has been struggling over an intricate manuscript by candlelight in a stone crypt. He gets up and shows his work to the fatherly abbot. "Benedict. Very nice. Now I would like five hundred sets of it."

Fear and rage show in Benedict's eyes. What will he do? He goes to his friend at the Xerox shop. Quick as a button he has five hundred sets at two pages a second. He returns to the abbot. "Here you are, the five hundred sets you asked for."

The abbot raises his eyes in fervent and pious thanks: "It's a miracle!"

during the 1950's intuition gave way to research in the planning behind commercials. The trend toward greater research grew during the Sixties, and in the Seventies threatened to squash creative guesses altogether. Money, really, was the reason sponsors demanded more careful planning before even letting a spot go on the air: as the costs per second to make, then to broadcast a spot—went up, nervous brand managers, those shepherds of an individual brand within the corporate flock, began to ask for scientific proof that a given campaign would work, often before anyone had seen it.

These demands got responses. Ad people started doing in-depth psychographics—studies purporting to report the psychological makeup of people who buy the sponsor's product. Graphs popped up on flip-chart stands when agencies were presenting their ideas to clients.

And testing has become a tense ritual. With so much cash riding on thirty seconds, sponsors have begun demanding that agencies test all commercials on sample audiences in vans near supermarkets or in theaters where computers can monitor brain waves, pupil movement, or sweat to see what audiences respond to. One company even offers cable TV to selected families if they will record their purchases every day; in this way, a major advertiser can find out whether its spots are actually changing anyone's buying habits, and it can compare the effectiveness of several different versions of a campaign. (Cost: $45,000 to $75,000 for a six-month study.) Other companies show small groups the spots on a TV set, then interview them or ask them to fill out questionnaires. Often half the audience forgets what brand was being advertised, and other commercials show a wide range of response: sometimes 90 percent of their viewers remember the brand, other times less than 15 percent do.

Of course, recall alone does not guarantee sales. But because it is easier to test recall than anything else, sponsors tend to judge the success or failure of their commercials on the basis of recall, particularly the levels found by Burke Marketing Research. Burke calls about 1600 people the day after a commercial has been shown. Usually about 200 folks have seen the show. Some people claim they remember the commercial, then show no idea what it was about. So the Burke interviewer asks what they saw, what they heard, to test for "related recall." Burke totals these items up under two headings: those that show the sales message got through, and those that simply show the person did see the commercial. On an average commercial, Burke finds that about 24 percent of the women watching will recall it; 22 percent of the men do. Anything higher than that pleases a client; anything less, and thunderclouds develop. If you use the product, you are slightly more likely to remember the commercial, it seems. Rich and middle-class consumers pay slightly more attention to commercials than poor ones do. The higher the education, the better the recall (25 percent of college grads recall commercials; only 20 percent of those who only finished grade school do.) Late night and prime time shows provide somewhat better recall than daytime shows (26 percent to 20 percent). And in general, people recall commercials somewhat better than they used to (24 percent overall in 1976 compared to 21 percent in 1967).

But advertisers want to be the best-remembered spot on the show, so they pore through Burke's verbatim recordings of interviews with the audience, looking for clues as to what worked and what missed. These responses can be disconcertingly vague, as: "There was a picture of several cans of fruit drink and somebody drinking it." Or, "A child was drinking this lime fruit drink." Or: "I remember a family in a kitchen. They had some of this drink. There was this big picture of the family in color and then, underneath, there was a whole lot of fine printing. It said something about containing vitamins and being good for the family's health." Here is what one man told Gallup & Robinson when they interviewed him about Stouffer's Lasagna: "It was cute; I liked it. It was the Mafia for dinner and they made Stouffer's Lasagna for the big boss. He likes it and all is well. I laughed. It was cute. I thought that I would like to try it. It increased my interest. I thought it was cute and it did stick in my mind." Now that's the kind of response that sends shouts down the halls of an ad agency.

When Jerry Della Femina scored a 75 percent recall on his singing cats commercial for Meow Mix—the highest score ever—he celebrated with a full-page ad in *The New York Times*. But even he pointed out that the commercial-makers were relying too much on Burke scores—and not sales—to decide whether or not a campaign was working. Other advertising executives agree. Theodore Dunn, director of research at Benton & Bowles, says, "One study showed that commercials that scored below average did not sell, but those above average sometimes sold and sometimes did not," and Marvin Honig, executive creative director at Doyle Dane Bernbach, is "concerned that the unique, the unusual, the controversial will be filtered out. In pre-test reports they often show up in a column titled 'negatives.' And negatives very often kill commercials. At Doyle Dane we've used humor and emotion very effectively to sell products. We try to touch people, to move them . . . the type of advertising you just feel in your gut can knock the market upside down." That's the kind of commercial the best ad-makers still strive for.

For all the research that corporations have done to find out who buys their products and why, for all the computer printout that has tabulated the results, for all the sociological jargon that has been Xeroxed, the resulting advertising strategies are often little more than what a good salesman would suggest after a year on the road. Market research prospers simply because people like the obvious to be confirmed before okaying a $3 million ad strategy.

One brand manager for a major soap—the member of the manufacturer's staff responsible for this particular product—wrote her ad agency this memo:

Who is buying my product now? Who else might be talked into buying it later? What conscious reasons do consumers give for buying my product? What unconscious impulses do shrewd shrinks think are really driving people to buy my product? What fantasies are associated with my product? What do people wish my product did for them? What promises, what suggestions, what claims can I make to persuade people to buy more?

The brand manager had just worked out a marketing plan for the next year, and she knew what volume of sales, what share of the overall soap market, what profits her brand would be expected to pull in. She would be judged mostly on her ability to expand her brand's share of the overall soap market, since profits are surprisingly hard to calculate brand-by-brand in a large conglomerate, and the volume of sales may be going up simply because everyone is buying more soap of every kind; expanding her share of the market, then, is the best measure of her personal pizazz, at least in upper management's eyes. So she turned to audience research to find new markets, new holes in the competition, new places to advertise. From her point of view, though, the results were fuzzy. "I found out how old the women were, how much money and schooling they had, and how clean they wanted to be. Some wanted lather, and others wanted complexion elements. After that, things got muggy. We were forced to go back to intuition after all—we looked to our agency's creative types to read all this crap, digest it, put it aside—and then come up with some great idea! The idea, that's what can make or break our strategy, and that comes, as often as not, from one person, working late, you know, maybe even trembling from too much coffee, looking out the windows at night, watching the cleaning ladies go through the offices across the street."

One idea—like Ivory Soap's "99⁴⁴/₁₀₀ percent pure" or Morton Salt's "When it rains, it pours." "Given a good idea, words and pictures become almost secondary in importance," says the Deep Throat of the advertising industry, Carl Wrighter. "They are used simply to convey the idea. A good idea can stand on its own. Most often, it is expressed as a short phrase; sometimes it is shown as a group of pictures. Why is a good idea so hard to find? First, because it must say either something new and different about the product or something about the product in a new and different way. Second, because it must say something about *you* that's new and different, or it must offer you a new and different point of view. It must be emotional in appeal, yet it must have a basic logic to it in order to make sense. And that's it."

But that's pretty tough. One way John O'Toole helps his employees at Foote Cone & Belding come up with savvy strategies for Clairol, Sunkist, and Dial involves answering this ticklish question: "Who is the individual human being that I must communicate with in order to effect a market of people who are attitudinally, demographically, emotionally like that person?" To understand that consumer, to empathize with a real individual, takes sympathy, wit, cynicism, compassion, wisdom—in brief, intuition. For Clairol Hair Setters, the main competition is curlers. Here's how O'Toole analyzes the potential purchaser: "Our prospect here, the individual we're talking to, is a woman anywhere between 25 and 40 who is concerned about her appearance. A woman who recognizes that she has to put in some time in order to look her best, but doesn't want to be caught in the act of doing so. What we want to leave her with is the memory that there is a good deal of shame and discomfort involved in being caught with curlers in your hair. In the effort to look beautiful in the end, you may be caught looking silly, and worse, in this woman's case, ugly. That is the strategy behind this commercial, entitled *Don't Get Caught with Your Hair Up*." We see women in curlers blush when men approach, cringe, retreat, while a woman says, "Get a Clairol Instant Hairsetter and the exclusive rollers for sets that are long-lasting and tangle-free."

For Loving Care Color-Lotion, the target is middle-aged women who notice gray hair creeping in. "Hate that gray? Wash it away!" In 1965 the actress in the ad said, "You know what I keep asking myself? How does Loving Care know which hair is gray when it colors only the gray?" Then the announcer gave a long explanation of how the product worked. Six years later the woman was still getting rid of her gray hairs, but she was now part of a larger drama: she was a woman going back to work. And the "scientific" explanation of how the product works had been abandoned in favor of a more "empathetic" appeal: "When the children started growing up and leaving home, I promised myself I wouldn't cry. Of course, I did. I guess I could have gone on sitting there getting a little grayer, a little sadder every year, waxing the floor again, cleaning the closet. Then one day I realized what I had to do over was me." Her voice changes, becoming brighter. Music appears. "So I went on a diet, I lost ten pounds, I went out looking for a job. I decided one thing I didn't need was gray hair." A real individual? Well, close to it— a composite with elements that could appeal to millions of women who have made similar decisions to reenter the job market.

Most strategists develop a USP (a Unique Selling Point) or a PA (Product Advantage), some reason you should buy their product, not Brand X. O'Toole and Clorox worked out this idea for Soft Scrub scouring powder: "The uniqueness in this product is that the construction in the granules provides less abrasion than is normally found in leading brands such as Ajax. Therefore, the competition is all of the existing scouring powders that do not offer this benefit. Who are we speaking to? A woman, middle demographics, interested in maintaining a clean household. The ultimate proof of a clean household is a shiny surface, particularly on stainless steel. What do we want her to know or understand? That there is a new kind of scouring powder, one that is going to clean just as effectively as those which she has been using, but because of this unique construction, it is not going to scratch, and it's going to leave more shine on her surfaces."

Procter & Gamble won't even release a new product without proving that it has a "Need for Being," that is, that thousands of consumers have revealed in interviews that they wish there were some product that could handle some particular problem.

Sometimes you take an established product, like Woolite, and point out that it can do much more than most consumers thought. Joe Brown, at Cunningham & Walsh, recalls saying, "Hey, look, it's not just for wool, despite what it's called. We said, 'Well, the next step from wool is knits. So we'll start talking knits.' And we kept

PILOT: Watch us shine.

AGENT: Watch us shine.

CHORUS: We're National the sunshine airline, watch us shine.

expanding and expanding to the point where we have even got people using Woolite in their washing machines." The commercial shows a woman coming out of the dry cleaner complaining about the high cost; her friend, or in other spots her husband, pulls a bottle of Woolite out of a paper bag.

N. W. Ayer did some research before writing ads for Nestlé's Souptime instant soup. The company found that housewives across the country felt good stock was essential in getting "that homemade kind of flavor." To emphasize the hominess and to verify the taste of their stock, they hired renowned actor and chef Vincent Price to taste it in his own kitchen, then plug Souptime with a smile. Within six months Souptime had outdone that year's goals for a share in the market.

Rubbermaid makes resilient garbage containers. Their big competition is trash cans. Their ad agency, Ketchum MacLeod & Grove, decided to crush the competition, literally. They put a Rubbermaid container next to a trash can in the back of a garbage truck. Then they pulled the lever. The slash bar slammed down on both products. We hear the gears grinding, the breaking; then they raise the bar. "The Rubbermaid container pops back into its original shape," says

the voice-over. "The metal can is a useless hulk." Rationally this is silly: you want a trash can to carry trash in, not to best a garbage truck. But irrationally this comparison makes sense: now we can see that rubber—far from being weak or flimsy—can actually be stronger than metal.

Sometimes a major company hits a series of reverses and calls on its ad agency for a new direction to draw customers back and to restore employee morale. During the early Seventies, for instance, National Airlines was making $20 million profit a year. Then it got hit by two long strikes; profits fell to around $3 million. And their "Fly me" ad campaign backfired when feminists organized a strong publicity campaign against such a sexy and sexist pitch. This dampened sales, too. So National hired John Anderson from American Express to "take apart our routes and put them back together again to get back our fair share of the market." His target: heavy users in the Sunbelt. "We're not after the mass-mass with this," he said. "We want to reposition ourselves as a carrier that appeals to the

NATIONAL AIRLINES Having retired the stewardesses who stripped down to bikinis, saying, "Fly Me," National now stresses what employees can do for the regular passenger.

heavy user, both for his business and his pleasure travel. The rub-off with the occasional user will come." Research showed that the most important factor in a heavy user's choice of an airline was the way employees treated passengers. So Anderson hired Ted Bates to do a new campaign focusing on captains, mechanics, baggage handlers, reservation clerks, and stewardesses. They walk around or work while babbling about the schedule and dependability. Over $7 million dollars put the corporate theme in newspapers; $3 million more put the message on TV. "Newspapers are our basic medium. Television is our reinforcing medium." National showed this commercial plus a twenty-nine-minute film of its staff at work to its 7,600 employees, saying, "We don't want to be the biggest airline; we want to be the best." The jingle:

> We're National the sunshine airline,
> Watch us shine, watch us shine,
> We're the sunshine airline, so
> Watch us shine, watch us shine.

Meanwhile, aiming at the same heavy user who demands personal service, American Airlines was rubbing in the fact that they were picked as the favorite airline by passengers surveyed by the Airline Passengers Association and Opinion Research Corporation. "Chosen Number One, twice in a row. That's not being lucky. That's being best!" American grinds that into the also-rans by showing their schedules tipping over like dominos: there goes United and Delta, now it's National, Eastern, and TWA. Only American's schedule stands up under competition. In another spot we see stewardesses lean into the camera to say, "Fly Braniff . . . Fly Eastern . . . Fly National." The announcer whispers that

AMERICAN AIRLINES Stacking its pamphlets up against the competition, American tips them over like a row of dominoes with its boast that one passenger association voted American. How American to be number one!

ANNOUNCER: If you were traveling anywhere in the United States,

The Airline Passengers Association asked that question

And the overriding reason was service.

and had your choice of any U.S. airline,

which airline would you choose,

and why?

in a recent survey of frequent fliers.

The answer?

More people chose American than any other airline.

Make American your number 1 choice and let us show you what we do best.

(SILENT)

(SILENT)

American Airlines won the competition, and when the statistics are over, we find a pretty stewardess pinning a big Number One on her outfit: she says, "Fly American . . . and let us show you what we do best."

The competitive spirit is so necessary to sales and advertising that some companies *invent* competition to spur profits. The phone company, which has little or no competition in most markets, took on the letter. AT&T had done research on users of phone service and discovered a group they labeled "The Budgeters"—people who are very aware of costs and don't feel much obligation to call anyone. "They prefer to write a letter rather than call long distance, but this is due primarily to the *perceived* cost of long distance. Letters are simply cheaper." Southwestern Bell Telephone, an AT&T subsidiary, evolved a strategy to make "The Budgeter" use the telephone: they would raise the value that these people saw in a long distance phone call, reminding them that compared to the cost of other products, long distance has stayed relatively cheap. In one commercial we see a car driving in heavy rain. "This man is going across town to visit his sister. He'll spend around a dollar sixty in gasoline getting there and back." We cut to a guy indoors, behind snug windows. "This man is going across the country to visit his sister." He dials and gets through while the driver is still slipping around corners. The seven-minute call costs 23 cents more. James Haake, vice president for marketing at Southwestern Bell, says, "During 1976, the company spent $3.2 million on a residence long distance advertising campaign. That campaign brought in an additional $32 million in revenue above what can be attributed to normal growth and increases in rates. We call this extra revenue 'stimulated' revenue."

C&P Telephone found that free calls for information were costing them too much in time and labor; they began charging for Directory Assistance. People resented having to pay for something that had been free, so the company embarked on an advertising campaign that pointed out that you can look a number up yourself. In one spot two guys go into separate phone booths. One looks up a number in a phone book, muttering, "Shoemaker, Shoemaker." The other calls information for Shoemaker, Margie. The guy who uses the book starts dialing. By the time the operator tells the second guy Margie Shoemaker's number, the first guy is telling Margie that she must remember him from the party. The other guy gets a busy signal. These commercials may have persuaded people not to spend extra dimes for information, thus trimming profits a bit, but they did what they were supposed to do, which was to help maintain public good will toward the company.

Getting rid of a bad image or unconscious fears can send sales up, so some corporations design strategies that will negate or overcome deep-seated worries that people have about their businesses. Lumber companies, for instance, find that the general public dislikes them because they chop down trees. St. Regis figured this was deep in the human psyche, and they went back to tree myths to suggest that somehow St. Regis was in league with the tree gods. Weyerhaeuser comes on like a gardener: they call themselves "the tree growing company," and in sixty-second commercials they show scientists working in labs to save young trees from deer (spray the baby trees with eggs; deer hate eggs) and to develop growth genes so that trees can "grow like crazy." In other spots we see Weyerhaeuser planting its one-billionth High Yield Forest seedling. My favorite stacks trees up against carrots, showing that trees take longer to grow but they both

WEYERHAEUSER   A corporate campaign designed to show that although the company protects its seedlings from deer, not even Bambi gets hurt.

A herd of deer can seriously stunt the growth of young trees. When the trees are small, every bite cuts down on the raw material for the next century. A bite of lumber. A gulp of plywood. Tomorrow's paper supply.

Dr. Illo Gauditz, Weyerhaeuser scientist, working with Dr. Katashi Oita, developed a way to discourage the deer.

An egg derivative. Dr. Gauditz found that deer hate eggs—poached, scrambled, or soft-boiled.

Result: A way to save wood resources. Without harming the Bambis of the world.

have deep roots and, seen from way above, they both look like grass.

Life insurance companies face similar problems since they only pay off after death. Mutual of New York and its agency, Marschalk, noticed that most insurance ads talk about the kids' future, college, retirement income but never mention that kicker: the insurance companies evidently believed that the public did not want to see a television commercial that talked about death. Instead of trying to deflect fear, as the paper companies do, Marschalk opted for confronting it. They decided to take a calculated risk and proclaim that "Death is the strongest possible argument for life insurance." The payoff after death, of course, is their unique product benefit, and that was uppermost in the consumer's mind, according to research. Marschalk worried that there might be some television code banning any mention of death, but evidently the censors had overlooked this. They worried that people might react with distaste, so they tested out their ideas in cartoon form. "We were still a bit nervous about the concept, but we were encouraged enough to go ahead with the testing. We had to be sure they were palatable to the public, and that the ideas behind the commercials were strong enough to justify spending a lot of money to turn those ideas into finished commercials. The results were extremely gratifying." People said they thought over their own insurance plans during the test-run. Commercials showed a family losing a cabin the father had worked for during his lifetime; a retired man who has plenty of time but not enough money to do anything (he should have bought life insurance); a woman and her son wandering around the office in which her dead husband used to work, lamenting that the company insurance plan did not really leave them much to live on. Several other insurance companies spend twice and thrice as much money on advertising, but MONY has managed to come in second or third in tests of advertising recall and awareness, thanks to these frightening but honest spots.

Howard Brod's jewelry firm, Wells-Benrus, faced another kind of sensitivity: "My feeling was that a lot of women want to get their ears pierced but have a vague anxiety—it might be more accurate to say a large anxiety with no fixed locus, rather similar to the anxiety women used to have about getting their hair dyed. I'm talking here about the older market, not the teenage market, who get their ears pierced automatically as a sort of puberty rite, a symbolic depucellage. Therefore to address the fear of pain, inconvenience, sex directly would be a mistake. The commercial was thus built upon a handy-dandy rationalization: get your ears pierced so you won't lose your earrings."

Sometimes the poor image a company suffers

under is its own fault. Too much calculation during the last campaign may have left a bad taste, so the company switches ad agencies and starts out with a new strategy. Snowmobiles had been selling 521,000 units, industrywide, in 1971; by 1976, after years of complaints about environmental impact, noise, and trespassing, sales were down to 195,000, and Bombardier, the manufacturer of the best-selling snowmobile, called SkiDoo, was suffering. Warren Daoust, the boss, called a big meeting with his staff and his agency, Sielaff/Johnson of Minneapolis. He wanted to look at every ad and article they could find about snowmobiles.

"It was doomsday," he says. "Everything was black and white and gray—nuts and bolts. You had to be a mechanic to understand what we were saying. There were color ads, and very sophisticated ones, too, but they were somber and dull. We were selling machines ridden by emotionless, faceless people. If anything, we were scaring people away from the sport."

Daoust put a million bucks into suggestive double entendre ads showing their spokesman skimobiling up to a cottage where a sexy woman leans out of an open door; the slogan is "Something hot on a cold winter night." The opening shots are aggressive: the snowmobile plunges up a ridge of powder, blasts a hole in it, roars over the camera; the SkiDoo makes a straight line across ridges of snow; the SkiDoo drives right up

MONY   Death came and emptied out his desk. Now Mom and the Son wander through the office, wishing Dad had taken out more insurance.

a narrow slot to the woman waiting there with wet lips. The announcer says, "Go 'doo it!"

More often the bad image a company has to combat comes from the competitor's ads, and a whole industry seems to squabble like generals in small countries. Car companies, for instance, often work out their strategies like war games, and the metaphor of war seemed particularly apt as the 1970's drew to a close: in four years, from 1970 through 1974, there were only thirteen new cars introduced; from the start of 1975 to the end of 1977 there were forty-eight more. Large cars got smaller; Ford brought back its European models to fight Japanese and German imports. Henry Ford II said that the smaller American cars "are going to give the imports one hell of a battle—we are going to push them right down to the shores," but Ford's biggest problem was simply to get people to come into their showrooms. So on TV they began showing the Fiesta breaking through the map of Europe, and customers, many of whom had never owned a Ford, came in just to see this marvel of territorial aggressiveness.

Not all new-car advertising was militaristic, though. Back in 1976 when AMC was ballyhooing its new Pacer, they hired Cunningham & Walsh to make the commercials. The first task: discover a unique selling proposition. "We positioned the Pacer as a wide small car, economical, and also roomy for a change," says Joe Brown. Their target audience was young, college-educated, upwardly mobile but not yet affluent, and they worked out a strategy to snare them.

Since people worried that AMC might leave them without service, several spots would prove how long the warranty lasted. Others would demonstrate what set Pacer apart from other wagons. The spots showed several cars trailing ropes; the Pacer drags its rope farther, and the announcer explains that the AMC warranty, called a Buyer Protection Plan, lasts longer and

KING: Mrs. Fitzhorton! It's on the way. Lou, bring everything . . . let's go!

on his giant creation, but

(SILENT)

ANNOUNCER: Fortunately the sandwich king had a new AMC Pacer.

The Pacer is wider than any other small car,

so he not only had room to work

he also got an incredibly stable

ride.

(SILENT)

The AMC Pacer. No other small car can make this sandwich.

(SILENT)

AMERICAN MOTORS Planned to demonstrate wide body and smooth ride, this spot slices its scene as carefully as the sandwich king does olives.

covers more than the competition's. The pictures are beautiful and weird; why would anyone drag a half-mile of rope down the highway, except to make a commercial?

In another spot, we drive along next to the driver, looking at the front of the Pacer, while the announcer says, "If you think this is an AMC Pacer, you're only half right." The camera pulls back and we see that in fact the man is driving half a car. "It's true it has a wide ride, rack and pinion steering, and lots of visibility. But it also has another half." Ah, here it comes. Apparently driverless, a rear end pulls into view, gradually catching up with its mate, while the announcer boasts about the cargo area. "It sets us apart from all other wagons."

The best of these Pacer spots, though, stresses the car's extra width. We see a man in a pizza parlor getting a phone call. "Mrs. FitzHorton, it's on the way," he says. He hangs up. "Move it. Get everything. Let's go. Hurry, quick, hurry. Don't forget the provolone." He and his assistant gather up all the makings for a giant hero sandwich and rush into the Pacer. The announcer says, "Fortunately because the Pacer is wider than any other small car, he had room to work on his giant creation." We hear opera on the sound track as he opens a very long loaf of Italian bread and starts larding in the salads. The announcer plugs the smooth, stable ride as our hero slices olives superthin. The car reaches Mrs. FitzHorton's and the butler, standing at the front steps, opens the door. The sandwich king gets out, sighs, and offers up his sandwich as if it were a cake.

Was AMC grateful for such amusing commercials? Not for long. All of these efforts helped to make the Pacer introduction one of the most successful new-car launches in auto history. But good advertising is not always enough to sustain a business when other forces are at work in the marketplace. By late 1976 public reaction against economy cars set in, and that worked in favor of the old-time luxury cars. Pacer got caught between supereconomy models, lower-priced imports, and scaled-down former luxury cars, and, despite all the planning, wit, and money spent on these spots, sales shrank. New management came in at AMC, and the company dropped its ad agency, looking for a new set of calculations.

Thus, behind every commercial, no matter how silly, lie hundreds of pages of research, strategy memos, and reasonable-looking plans. When we hear a claim or see a fast demonstration, we may not notice it, but some copywriter has probably spent hours figuring out who the most likely consumers are for his product, what would motivate them to buy, what might make them hold back, and what gimmick could overcome their hesitation.

Retreating to higher ground, some larger corporations—particularly those with many different product lines—choose to put their money into corporate ads. These ads keep the stock buoyant and reassure executives and employees that even though their products do not show up in the supermarket, their corporation is nationally important. Furthermore, a consistent campaign can build up a favorable image, like a bank reserve, to be drawn against when popular opinion turns against the company or its industry. A few of these corporate ads are really catalogues of the many items one company sells. For instance, a disembodied voice interrupts one man who is sitting in a stuffed chair reading: "Sir, what do you feed your rabbit?" The man looks up: "I don't have a rabbit." But suddenly there is a rabbit right next to him, sniffing his chair. "Uh-oh. Now I need rabbit food." The announcer suggests Purina Rabbit Chow. "Now, what about your monkey?" A monkey appears. "Your horse? Goat? Hen? Veal? [Sic.] Pigeon? Dog?" We can see, by now, that Ralston Purina makes a whole lot of animal feed.

AMF makes bicycles, boats, bowling balls, golf clubs—and they wanted to plug the whole corporation in one spot. How? At Benton & Bowles the team decided to do a cartoon called "How AMF Made the Weekend." The story: "One day Monday came to AMF." Monday is painted blue. Nobody likes him. Everyone is grumpy when he or she comes to work. So AMF made the weekend, during which people can use Voit Balls, Hatteras Yachts, Sunset Boats, Ben Hogan Golf Equipment, and so on. In sixty seconds they recap every major product line within a unified story.

Most real corporate ads, though, rise even higher above the battle. In fact, some seem to be so high-toned, preachy, and abstract that no one could disagree. Most campaigns wag and waffle, too, running for six months, then dropping away as market pressures build up and the corporation diverts money to a particular brand. Many corporations forget to mention their products, to take a stand on issues they know bother consumers, or to admit error. Alex Kroll, president of Young & Rubicam, USA, thinks ads that show a corporation as unstoppable and inevitably successful may frighten people, implying that the company is powerful but oblivious. Kroll suggests ads that allow for feedback from the public, as in Ford's campaign ("We listen.") or Gulf's, which lists phone numbers to call "to get your facts from, to bitch to, to talk to." Arco even published an outside audit of its social performance, including the fact that its liabilities included an all-white, all-male management, a limited effort to educate consumers on conservation, and indifference to the sufferings of dealers whose service stations get closed. "Did the world fall on Arco? No, not at all. My own feeling is that Arco rose in public estimation," says Kroll.

In 1973 International Telephone and Telegraph commissioned the research firm of Yankelovich, Skelly and White to find out what people thought about the company. It turned out that many people did not even know the firm existed. "The awareness scores were remarkably low, considering that in 1972, ITT was the ninth largest industrial company in the nation," says an ITT executive, John Lowden. "That low awareness really surprised us. We'd been running a corporate campaign right along through our corporate agency, Needham, Harper & Steers, and the reactions we were getting were very good. But this print campaign had been aimed at too narrow a target audience. Business, finance, government, the academic world, the so-called influentials." To broaden the audience, they decided to switch media dollars into TV. "We needed both TV's reach and its speed of communication. Also, we knew that many of ITT's products and services—some of them highly complex and very unfamiliar to the average consumer—would have to be seen in action to be understood." And on TV, they decided to stress ITT's constant research and development and its world-wide scattering of subsidiaries and branches.

"Could we really fill that identity void? Could we create the kind of confidence in our company and its policies which would put a lot of rumors and irresponsible allegations to rest?" ITT began tracking attitudes in households with incomes of $15,000 or more. They made commercials showing the mannequin that can be used in teaching heart surgery instead of carving up a human, the antiskid devices that keep cars from crashing into unsuspecting cameramen, cables laid underwater in Norway, fellowships for students to go to Europe for a year, and a device so that people suffering from night-blindness can see dimly in the dark. Awareness rose from 34 percent in January 1974 to 59 percent in July 1975. "So the identity void is being filled on our terms. Awareness of ITT—favorable awareness—is, now approaching that of other major corporations." People began to associate these ideas with ITT: "develops new products," "leads in technology," "makes quality products," "cares about the public," "protects U.S. jobs." Worried that people might think they were not making enough profit from such

public-spirited enterprises, ITT launched a second set of commercials focusing on more obviously money-making innovations: fiber optics, continuous remote control of trains, and new techniques of animation.

Most of these commercials shared one other feature: they brought news. Each told the viewer something most people did not know before, unless they happened to be experts in ophthalmology or engineering. Each spot worked better than the evening news show to provide information. And after six months the number of people who figured ITT was a good stock to buy went from 52 percent to 65 percent. It's enough to make a capitalist pat his pinstripe and grin.

Conclusion: when you see a commercial you like, ask yourself, Am I part of the target audience for this product? Are they aiming at my age, my class, my psychological reasons for buying this kind of product? If you feel pinpointed, you may be caught in the cross hairs of calculation and research.

In television advertising, as in war, no strategy can succeed without surprises. And that is where personality counts. Now the writers and art directors have to come up with an original idea—part visual, part verbal, part something else—an idea that sums up the key points in the strategy worked out by the corporation and the researchers, satisfies every wish, tells enough of the truth to pass for news, and spouts enough malarkey to make you buy, steering between the whirlpool of overdone production and the rocks of a drab announcer. The idea is subtler than anything research turns up.

It can come from a chance conversation, as when Howard Cohen and Bob Pasqualina went to a big dinner after they had finished an Alka-Seltzer commercial, and someone said, "I can't believe I ate the whole thing." Cohen's wife said, "That would make a great commercial." It did.

An idea can come from a stray word association: Al Coleman was working for Barickman Advertising when a friend drove him to the airport and said as he left, "Remember the guys back home." Coleman explains, "He knew a number of people I knew and was reminding me to think of them. But later I associated his remark with Guy's Foods, my client, mainly for the Guy's Potato Chip advertising. I worked on it as a slogan and came up with, 'Don't forget the Guys,' which is stronger than 'Remember the Guys.' Then within about a week I presented it to Guy Caldwell, president of Guy's. He liked it. It's been there ever since, on all our advertising."

Ed Buxton, the adman who retired to run *Ad Day,* an inside-dope tip-sheet for the business, says that lots of good ideas come out of curiosity. At Ally & Gargano, for instance, they ran a series of spots showing kids giving lame excuses for their toys being broken. One child said, "An elephant stepped on it." Someone wanted to see what that would look like—and the result was that commercial in which an elephant rests its foot on a Tonka truck. Janet Wolfe, at the William Esty agency, wanted to know what would happen to a rose if you put it in dishwater suds with Vel. The rose held up well; the ads sold Vel.

A great idea has both verbal and visual components: a slogan that evokes a scene, a picture that makes the viewer recall the brand name and claim. The Jolly Green Giant is such an idea: a symbol, a character, a trademark. The three elves—and their names, Snap, Crackle, and Pop —leap out of Rice Krispies with an idea. It was an idea that created an invisible shield around anyone who brushed with Colgate; that put a tiger in Esso's tank; that turned Mercury Cougar into a purring sex kitten at "the sign of the cat." And perhaps because a big idea sets the mind moving back and forth between image and description, between vision and words, a commercial with a big idea can outdistance a routine, mainly verbal ad in sales response by 15 to 1, according to studies by the Association of National Advertisers.

And the big ideas that sell often seem to do so because they perform a fast flip-flop on our expectations. "Which will last longer, your five thousand dollar car" (we see an old car being junked) "Or our car, that sells for about a buck?" (a hand opens, revealing a tiny Matchbox car). Or we see a fuzzy picture of cars while the announcer says, "Our cars need no gas, never get a flat, and are guaranteed for ten thousand. . ." (we have pulled back far enough to see the hand) "pushes." The common chain of commercials, though, offers few surprises. Most wine ads show misty scenes in which a couple drink the right brand and begin to kiss. Most soap ads show incredible foam and lather all over the shoulder, the chin, the knee, the shower stall. Most shampoo ads show the fluffy results by having a tall model do neck twists in slow motion, lifting, blowing, swirling her hair. Most car ads show medium shots of the car on curves, straightaways, hills, in sun and darkness, but almost none ever show what the highway looks like from the driver's seat. You get pretty pictures, but no new idea.

The startling ideas, like the Xerox monk saying, "It's a miracle!," seem to come from people who want to shock, to mesmerize, to make sure we remember. Often, top writers of commercials are like street-wise, smart-aleck kids who like the thrill of saying things that no one else has dared to say before. They run perilously close to disaster in some campaigns, but often their very originality scores—very big—overnight. That gives them a taste for power, and they begin to talk like prizefighters.

George Lois, one of the most personable of these creative stars, says, "What you can do with TV commercials is magic. You can make a product famous instantly. What's funny about most ad agencies is that they don't understand that. I say that what I do is famous advertising. Most big agencies don't know how to plan that, so they go back to the Harvard Business School guys, they sit down, and they figure it out.

"I was on *The David Susskind Show* with some ad guys the other day, and he said, 'Well, what is advertising supposed to do?' And one of them says, 'It gives information.' And that's really what most of them think it does, you know—take the good points, and present them to the people, and leave it to their good judgment. I mean, a lot of critics of advertising think we're all hustlers and charlatans; you kidding? They're not sharp enough to be good hustlers. Hustlers I love.

"Most of these guys are straight information-givers and information-getters and research types.

ALKA-SELTZER A classic, created by Howard Cohen and Bob Pasqualina after a chance conversation, this spot shows how a great idea can become a folktale within a month.

HUSBAND: I can't believe I ate that whole thing.

HUSBAND: I can't believe

ALKA-SELTZER NEUTRALIZES ALL THE ACID YOUR STOMACH HAS CHURNED OUT.

ANNOUNCER: Alka-Seltzer neutralizes all the acid your stomach has churned out.

WIFE: You ate it, Ralph.

HUSBAND: I can't believe I ate that whole thing.

WIFE: No, Ralph, I ate it!

I ate that whole thing.

WIFE: Take two Alka-Seltzer.

SOUND: PLOP, PLOP . . . FIZZ.

For your upset stomach and headache, take Alka-Seltzer, and feel better fast.

WIFE: Did you drink your Alka-Seltzer?

HUSBAND: The whole thing.

"I told the guy, 'You and I are in different businesses. I spray poison gas.' "

His poison gas, though, smells like perfume to the sponsors. And part of the scent is Lois's originality, which he insists on. "There aren't many people who try to do what I do. Everything I do is try to come up with a big, strategic, tactical idea. I get the idea and say it to the client, he should faint. He should almost throw you out of the room. Or else you ain't got much of an idea. There's nothing memorable about it.

"A lot of people get interesting ideas, but they don't try hard enough. I call commercials the ultimate drag race. Here's a cliff; if you go that far and stop, you're chicken; if you go this far, you got some guts; if you stop at the edge, you're the winner. If you go over, it's a fiery death. You just overdid the idea, it was too much, too grating. But if you don't want to play the game, don't press on the gas.

"Look, I could literally work with hammer and nail—I could nail down a camera in most cases, because the thought and the strategy and the thinking and the imagery and what's being said is so dramatic, so to the point, so slightly insane or slightly outrageous that I stop you with visual imagery or what is being said, rather than tricks and effects, or going to Japan to shoot an eighty-thousand-dollar commercial. When you come to a ten-second commercial, I simply had Joe Louis saying, 'I just want to say one thing: Edwards and Hanley, where were you when I needed you?' You can't beat it because of its humanity.

"With everything I do, you've got to look at it when it comes on and say, 'What the hell is going on?' There is something in that first couple of seconds so that when you look at it, you say, 'I better not get the beer now.' "

Lois is athletic and relaxed; he does his homework, but he does not overvalue it. "After you analyze the market and what the company's all about, and analyze the competitors and what they're doing, and talk to people and get some of the research, and after learning about something for a couple of weeks until you don't want to learn any more, then you say, how can I sell this?

"How do I get kids on the street to talk about the commercial, to use the slogan? It all comes

after that thinking—then you get the big idea, and you say, boy, I'm gonna knock everybody dead with that. I usually end up doing something hypnotic or something slightly screwy."

He motions to six storyboards on foam-core boards next to him. "I'm working on something now for a cigarette modifier. I call it Snake Woman. When you press this little machine, two little prongs come out and bite into the cigarette; it's a ventilating system, which literally works 97 percent of the time, blah blah blah. So I've named the product Snakebite. That's the big idea. And I create a Snake Woman. This woman comes out of the smoke—and I got you by the balls. Another one, she comes up with a cigarette, and six guys come up with lights, and she says, 'Fools, I'm not going to smoke it. I'm going to bite it.' I have one where there's this fantastic woman, and a guy says, 'You've come a long way, baby,' and Snake Woman tells the other woman, 'That's the way you show your

EXCELLO   First impressions attract us, then confirm our faith in that cliché: easy but magical, this spot sells clean shirts.

independence, taking up men's filthy habits?' I got you.

"It's all from the idea of calling this the Snakebite. Snakebite removes cigarette's poisonous venom. That's the big idea. And when Snake Woman comes on, I got you, I literally got you, there's no way you can possibly turn off, whether you like it, hate it, adore it; I got everybody talking about it. I got Adam and Eve, and she slides in and says, 'Fools, you had a paradise on earth until you took up smoking.' Now that's hypnotic. I ain't doing cinematography—cinematography is bullshit."

Instead of fancy cinematography, Lois thought up the Pontiac choirboys, in which dealers sing the theme song, and the Olivetti Girl, in which he turned Joe Namath into a cute secretary. "With Olivetti I went to purchasing agents and said, 'Have you ever looked at Olivetti typewriters? You ever talk to a salesman?' 'Yeah, oh, they come here all the time, they drive me crazy.' I wasn't sure about their sales force, so I asked, 'Why don't you try them?' 'If I take away her IBM and give her an Olivetti, the girl will go crazy.' So I have to romanticize the typewriter to the girls, and then some of these guys are going to buy it. I used twelve girls on the Olivetti Girl. They tripled their sales. Then after a guy bought two machines, I'd run a little ad in the paper, saying, 'Joe Blow Inc. now has two Olivetti Girls,' and I'd put in their names, and they'd call up and order two more. The National Organization for Women came and they complained that I didn't show female executives and male secretaries. I said, 'What a commercial!' So I got Joe Namath, who I knew could type, and I got a female exec at a cosmetic company, and I made the commercial. You know the old story—every boss is trying to make the secretary? I just turned the tables on that. The N.O.W. people just looked at that commercial, got up, sneered, and walked out."

Faced with a product named QWIP, a telecopier from Exxon, he found that the Exxon salesmen were embarrassed to use the name because they sounded like the cartoon character Elmer Fudd when they said it. "So I got to figure out how to make that name fun and famous. Ninety-nine percent of the creative people in this city, if I told them my idea, they'd probably walk away from me. That QWIP, it's a crazy word, so I do a whole QWIP QWAZY campaign. I made up a guy who talks like Elmer Fudd, called Quentin Quibble. Quentin Quibble is quazy about QWIP. This girl is going to airmail something, he says, 'Don't qwy it, QWIP it.' People never forget that. We went in there with an awareness of one percent among business people; we came out with a seventy-two-percent awareness."

Words are important to Lois's ideas. "I've never done commercials that didn't have words in them. I'll say the name of a product eight times. I'm working on a thirty-second commercial for a new magazine, and I say the name of the magazine seventeen times in those thirty seconds. "I design my commercials so I keep coming at you. Guys who design commercials where you don't hear, I think they're crazy. You know what a second costs on TV—two to four thousand dollars; you're not going to piss it away. I don't need mood to get you into it."

With Lois, then, personality makes his style tough. He has the guts and the rough strength of a fighter on vacation. And he loves his own magic. In his book, *The Art of Advertising*, he put together a dazzling scrapbook of work for (among others) Off Track Betting (the New York Bets), Pirelli Tires, Bobby Kennedy, Puss

---

MATCHBOX   Uncle Sam and march music lead us to expect an ad for savings bonds; then he opens his hand, and we realize, with surprise and relief, he's offering us a toy car for a buck.

"A good car for only a buck."

'n' Boots (Yogi Berra talking to a cat), Maypo (ball players whine, "I want my Maypo"), REA Express ("Hi yo, REA, away!"). At $45 a copy, it's little wonder that Lois even makes up his own ads to sell his book by mail.

Other admen content themselves with great lines. "Gee—I could have had a V-8." "Get Wise." "We do it all for you." These work their way into the conversation, like, "You deserve a break today," and "When it rains, it pours." Morton's Salt and McDonald's know the value of a jingle you may like to repeat. Good slogans are fingerlicking good. They're mountain grown, and natural. They put their strength where the dirt is. Like Birds' Eye, they've got quality in their corner. And, like Eveready Alkaline Energizers, they last and last. You can be sure if it's

a slogan. Slogans are the ones to have if you're having more than one. Get me one while you're up. With a name that's a slogan, it has to be good.

Real ideas, though, go beyond phrases to create imaginary situations. For Meow Mix, Della Femina Travisano has cats call up the grocer, ordering the catfood by name. Playing on those detergent commercials in which housewives from cities across the country ask for one brand, and toying with their own brand name, claiming that every cat that meows is asking for Meow Mix, they show us nine cats purring. "We asked cats all over America what catfood they loved best." Each cat meows over a logo giving the name of some city. The last one barks instead —it's from Brooklyn. "Meow Mix . . . nine out of ten cats ask for it by name." And then they spoof their own campaign in another spot in which a British-sounding announcer says, "Please pay attention to this commercial because there's going to be a test afterwards. This is an ordinary meow." The cat meows. "It could mean anything from 'I love you' to 'It's about time you changed my litter box.' Now this is a Meow Mix meow." The cat gives exactly the same sound. "It can only mean one thing: a request for Meow Mix catfood." Now comes the test; the cat meows, and the announcer says, "Which meow was that?" So now they have your cat spouting their slogan every time it gets hungry. Now that's a real idea.

Reva Korda, creative head of Ogilvy & Mather, laughs at the word *creativity*. "What a pompous, pretentious word it is! I like the word *copy* so much more. The best title in the advertising business is Copy Chief. Copy *is* the core of the business. Writing, not film, not graphics, makes ads work," she feels. "Writing is the key kernel in any of the great ideas; with words, the idea grows into a scene, a little drama, a short film."

Naturally, acres of advice have piled up around the creation of commercials. Most of the suggestions are either stupid or trivial. Most textbooks on commercial writing tell you that there are different genres—the problem/solution commercial, the slice of life, the demonstration, the testimonial, the interview, the spokesperson—and that you should know your product, know your consumer, stick to the overall strategy, and stay within the guidelines published by the National Association of Broadcasters. Right. Getting this advice is like having an academic tell you how to write a novel. It turns out to be easier to list sins than virtues. Harry Wayne McMahan, who makes a living picking the 100 Best Commercials every year for *Ad Age,* says the biggest problems are these: you can't tell why the commercial begins where it does, or why it

ends; it does not stand out from the clutter on either end; there is no one key visual that we can remember; the camera angles are too weird to let us see the golf ball; the cast got too big (three is plenty); and the commercials were not re-echoed in print ads or the spots not repeated often enough.

What it comes down to is that the best ad-makers develop their own styles, their own approaches, and the mediocre ones just do what has been done before, like the people who do "pools" of commercials. A pool is a series of variations on one basic idea, such as the innumerable Palmolive spots with Madge the Manicurist. Jerry Della Femina and Ron Travisano make unique spots by joking around with their products. When Airwick came out with a twin-pack, they sent a camera and interviewer into supermarkets asking, "Would you like to have twins?" One woman laughs: "At my age!" Two teenage girls blush, and one says, "I'd like to get married first." Of one couple, the wife says yes, the man, no. Coming out the door of the laundry, a man says, "Why would I want to have twins?" Behind him are nine children. Such humor may attract our attention because the authors seem to be joking about their own product—the reverse of what we expect in a commercial.

In a companion piece for Airwick's small-space air deodorizers that you can stick on anything, we go back to the grocery, where a clerk says, "Attention, shoppers, this is a stick up." The customers raise their hands. Then we see the clerk hold up a package of the product. An old woman leans forward in a taxi, and says, "Sonny, this is a stick up." The burly cabby says, "Don't hurt me." And in the supermarket checkout line, a woman checker looks at a guy with a gun in his pocket and says, "Don't be silly. That's your finger. *This* is a stick up!" And she shows him the product. The laugh beats the robber; in the same way, humor can deflate consumer resentment and introduce us to a product we didn't particularly want to hear about.

So can a good jingle—but only by certain writers. Steve Karmen, who wrote "When you say Bud, you've said it all" and "Wrigley Spearmint gum, gum, gum" plus "Pick a Pack of Juicy Fruit" and "See Beneficial First, toot, toot," always tries to work the name of the company in once every five seconds. Using simple harmonies, he rarely lets the music overwhelm the voice, and sponsors love him. But many other composers like the music too much. You hear them play and you think it's a song, not a commercial. Language gets smashed, so we lose any interplay between the picture and the point. Sally Oppenheim, who does lyrics for a jingle house, stresses that the best jingles are designed to be done in pieces so that the announcer can come in at certain points and override them with spoken words, then let the song rise to the surface again for some tag like, "If you think it's butter, but it's not, it's new Chiffon."

But veteran adman Tony Schwartz ridicules both jokes and jingles. From his point of view, jingles break up the rhythm of real speech and thereby ruin the meaning (if there was any). Furthermore, a jingle is no substitute for a scene that evokes feelings rather than teaches phrases. Mere verbal recall is not enough for Schwartz. He wants to set off an atom bomb in your unconscious, using what you already know and feel to work for his product or politician. He sees commercials as stimuli, not content; prods, not arguments, as he points out in his book *The Responsive Chord:*

The association could be made by having a woman, not necessarily a real housewife, reacting to a stopped-up sink in a *believable* way. Believability is more important than reality. I am not talking about a Josephine the plumber type. If the advertiser can render a deep commercial on the feelings of a believable woman after she unstopped a sink that had been troubling her for several days, a real experience

CABBIE: Get wise, Mac, get wise.

KIDS: Get wise, get wise!

CHARLIE CHAN: Get wise, get Wise potato chips!

WISE FOODS Such scenes help us to memorize the slangy phrase; when we get the idea, we buy potato chips.

is created for the listener or viewer, and it will be stored permanently in his or her brain. When the consumer sees the product in the store, whether he or she consciously remembers it or not, the product may evoke the experience of the commercial. If that experience was meaningful, and there is a need, the consumer is likely to buy the product.

Notice the Pavlovian behaviorism implicit in Schwartz's description of a commercial's effect: he intends to implant an electrode in our mind, timed to go off the moment we see the product. Perhaps Schwartz would be gratified to see consumers actually drool in the aisle. We can see the essential humorlessness, the tone deafness of Schwartz's heavy ideas in the spot he did attacking Goldwater during the 1964 election: a little girl plucking flowers, an atomic explosion, and LBJ's voice in the background sounding as if he were reading the Bible, saying, "Either we must love each other or we must die." No reasoning here. Very simple, even sentimental, thinking, based on research that showed voters worried that Goldwater might start a nuclear war. Two pictures and one drippy phrase: it killed Goldwater's already shaky candidacy.

Part of our American unconscious must *like* getting hit in the face with the big idea. We have, it seems, been trained to think that complex issues can and should be reduced to slogans. But while commercials have refined this habit, we now expect that the gist of any decision—war, peace, election, purchases of soap—can best be presented in a few emotionally wrenching pictures, with one sentence that sounds as if it sums up the point. Our imagination responds to the picture of an admiral on the deck of his ship saying, "Damn the torpedoes. Full speed ahead." We like Harry Truman pounding his desk saying, "The buck stops here."

An aggressive personality, then, with punchy ideas, can often set off sales and in turn make the writer rich. Charlie Moss, for instance, has done some of the funniest and saddest commercials on the air, and his career as a whole stands as a model for most admen; he's done what they would like to have done, and faster, and he's done it in his own way. Remember the violent Mom who chases her kid around the house to make him brush with Gleem? And the guy who stole the trade secret about that new American Motors car—and got a javelin in the chest? Those were his ideas.

Moss had something of the smart aleck in him in some of his early spots, such as one in which we see a building superintendent getting told off by a bitchy tenant. Then a businessman in a fedora walks in. "So the plumbing is on the blink, and the neighbors have threatened to riot, eh, Mr. Polanski?" Polanski nods: "That Mrs. Vanderkopf in Six K, she gave me headache, and such heartburn." The Fedora has an answer: Alka-Seltzer. They go into the boiler room, and he explains to the bewildered super: "Liquid is a fast way to get to your pylorus. It's like an escape valve in your stomach. Mrs. Vanderkopf gets nasty and it doesn't work right. Gas and acid can't get out." But with Alka-Seltzer—Fedora demonstrates by letting the steam out of the boiler, ruining the pressure for the day. "Look what you've done to my boiler!" wails Polanski. Fedora is unmoved: "No, Mr. Polanski, think what I've done for your pylorus." In another spot a man is stuck by the side of the road, changing a flat. He's in a bad mood, and he has a headache and heartburn. The same smart-ass in the fedora shows up, saying that Alka-Seltzer relieves that feeling of pressure, that it works just like letting air out of a tire—and he lowers the last tire before he drives off.

The small but telling fact that Moss's superintendent has the same name as a film director (Roman Polanski) betrays this writer's deep affection for tough-guy flicks. He did a Humphrey Bogart ad for the Rebel. A Bogie look-alike, wearing a Panama hat, pulls up to a

ANNOUNCER: Why put up with a noisy muffler?
HOBO: Midasize that car!

COP: Midasize it!

WORKERS: Midasize that car!

desert corral, where some Mexicans are sitting. "Hey, Mac, this here the Baja?" He even *sounds* like Bogie. The Mexicans respond, "You loco, señor, you goin' to drive that 'onk of tin through the Baja? Hahahahah." Bogie says, "She ain't no hunk of tin. She's the Rebel. Tough as any car you ever seen." Shades of *African Queen*. Bogie spins gravel and gets out of town while the announcer says that "The savage Baja is a menace to everyone on wheels." On the road, Bogie's buddy says, "Joe, it's too rough, we've got to turn back," but Bogie says, "The Rebel is like a dame, you got to have faith in her." They drive by a car littered with buzzards and reach the beach. The announcer boasts, "If a Rebel could make the Baja last year, it should take anything you can dish out." Bogie pats the car, "You're good, really good."

Moss also wrote a soap opera for Safeguard, reducing one regular consumer to hysterics. We see a guy wearing a towel, asking in paranoid terror: "Louise, there's a strange soap in my soap dish. Where's my Safeguard?" Louise is calm, ordinary: "Well, they were all out at the store, so I got something else." She does not understand. "What are you trying to do to me, Louise?" Louise shrugs. His voice sharpens, goes up an octave: "You know I've got that big meeting today. I need that old confidence going in. I'm no good without it. I won't have that cool, confident feeling that my Safeguard gives me, Louise. You happy, Louise? You killed it, you killed my confidence." Louise says, "You're getting hysterical over nothing," but she does not know business life. "Louise, you go out into that jungle, and you'll know what they do to you. They tear you to pieces." It's no use—poor hubby goes down the front walk shaking at every joint.

MIDAS Charlie Moss made up a new word, then created scenes to pound it into us.

INSTRUCTOR: Let's see if we can find first. No, that's not it.

Believe me, it's in there somewhere.

ANNOUNCER: It's hard to hurt a Rebel.

Driving schools use more of our cars

than any other kind.

How does it feel, your first time out, Mr. Moss?

Mr. Moss?

Mr. Moss!

INSTRUCTOR: Look out for that truck.
STUDENT: What truck?

INSTRUCTOR: Behind that bus.
STUDENT: What bus?

STUDENT: Should I turn the wind-shield wipers on?

ANNOUNCER: Looks like the Rebels will outlast the teachers.

In another tearjerker, Mom and Pop are watching TV when Daughter comes in. She is crying. "Honey, what happened? What did he do?" say the concerned parents. Pop looks ready to strangle Daughter's date. She begins to talk: "He said I needed . . ." but she can't say it. She holds up a box of Safeguard. Pop explodes: "Safeguard! Kid takes my daughter out then says we got perspiration odor. That little punk. I'll tear him into pieces. Go get the soap, Edna." Edna fetches their soap. He checks it against Safeguard, goes out to the boy. Pop comes back crying, too. "I'm afraid the boy makes a lot of sense, Edna, he makes a lot of sense." They all hug.

Moss was a child actor, off and on, and his commercials tend to be written as dramatic scenes, brief movies. One of his funniest shows a driving school instructor suffering as his inept students drive up on curbs, back out across traffic, crunch the car on both sides. This Perils of Pauline script supposedly proves how much abuse the Rebel and the driving instructor can take, but its real point seems to be entertainment.

Moss's trump suit is writing. And he sets up most scenes to introduce or reinforce a phrase he wants us to remember. For Midas mufflers he invented the word *Midasize*. We see various people our car is offending with its loud broken muffler, and they all yell, "Midasize it." That is like writing your own dictionary entry. He also thought up scenes in which people break their extra-long Benson and Hedges cigarettes and light cigars with a "Flick of my Bic." These offer actors great opportunities for the exaggerated gesture—three-second cameo roles. In these spots we often see three or four scenes, then a shot of the product by itself, then one final joke.

At first Moss was just a hotshot writer. "I was the writer on American Motors. That was probably the most exciting campaign I've worked on in my whole life. Because essentially I'm a ham—

AMERICAN MOTORS   This funny spot by Charlie Moss shows how much mistreatment the American Motors Rebel can absorb; it's called "Driving School."

I perform better when I feel people are watching. And the ad world was really watching that account, because American Motors was supposed to be ready to go out of business, yet here they were employing a hot, quote creative unquote agency which had not yet proved itself in big business. On top of that, *Life* decided to make a feature story out of the campaign, so they followed us everywhere. We got started on the account July 4th, and we had to have finished commercials on the air in the middle of September. For our kind of work, which is extremely involved with casting and dialogue and dramatics, that's a very short time.

"We practically could do what we wanted, American Motors had so much faith in us; we shot the *Driving School* commercial without a storyboard, and the client said, 'I don't think it's going to be funny,' and I said, 'Just trust us, it'll be funny.' They would go ahead and spring for eighty thousand dollars to make this a one-minute commercial because they felt we would deliver, and we did.

"After we did American Motors we seemed to get every big account going. We did the Million Dollar Bonus for TWA. They said, 'Look, we have nothing new to sell, we can't afford to put in electronic whatevers, we can't do anything different, we can't paint the planes, we can't change the uniforms. But we need something that will excite people, we need something that will get our employees to give better service, to try our line again, because service has slipped.' So we went away, and we thought for a number of days, and came up with this idea; what if we gave away a million dollars to employees who give superior service? That was the basic idea, and once we had that, and once they bought

STEWARDESS: Coffee, tea . . . or a flick of my Bic?

that, we made these 'What-If' commercials. Some fabulous commercials. Most people have never seen them. But as little films, they're some of the best I've ever seen. There's one called *Locker Room.* The baggage retrieval department head comes into the locker room after a particularly successful flight and tells the guys their baggage handling wasn't good enough. One of the guys makes an excuse. He says he was carrying a dog cage but the dog bit him, and that's why he had to slow down. The foreman says, 'Special Dog Cage drill, tomorrow morning, seven o'clock.' It shows how hard people will work for you, and for a million bucks. And there's one called *Ticket Agent* with a nagging wife. From the time the guy gets up in the morning, all through breakfast, all the way out to the car, she's nagging him about winning this bonus, 'Do the right thing, be nice to people, put them in the right seat.' There's the porter who helps the old man into the terminal, saying his name is Bud Jones a hundred and fifty times so the man will remember his name. The bonus was a hard fact, something TWA employees could win, and we dramatized it in human terms with a specific dramatic idea."

Ideas do backfire sometimes. Moss figured out

BIC Another phrase that gives its product a fillip; the spot shows us some scenes in which the phrase sounds suggestive, ridiculous, or pathetic, by turns; we learn the trick.

one campaign for Sunoco in which the company would do favors for anyone who showed up on the credit card printout as a regular customer. "That turned out to be an impossibility from a legal standpoint and a hundred other ways." But Moss kept the basic quid pro quo idea and turned it into a slogan for a garageman to say at the end of a spot: "I take care of my friends." Moss explains, "That meant that if you come in and buy gas from me, I'll know you are one of my friends, so if you break down, I'll come out and get you, no flim-flam about it. When you come in for a valve job, you'll be sure I'll take care of your car just a little more than I would a stranger's. You would have this credit built up. The idea was a sensational one from this motivational point of view. You could believe that in fact the guy would. What happened was the gas shortage. Just before we started to shoot those commercials, they came to us and said, 'Hey, look, we're going to have a gas shortage, and "I take care of my friends" is going to look very strange during a gas shortage.' It implied something it wasn't meant to imply. So we had to change the line, and even the thrust of the campaign subtly. It was not as hard an issue any more."

After these successes, Moss got bucked upstairs to become creative director, supervising other people's writing, then vice chairman. He still did commercials, but as a manager he became more and more involved in other people's work, and he ended up doing only the stuff no one else wanted to do. Had he changed? Yes, he says. "For the better, I think. I'm not nearly as temperamental or as precious or as jealous about what I do, because I've seen it from the other side so often. I'm much more interested in the idea or result than I am in the particular details of how they're accomplished. Coming up with an interesting line, or funny dialogue, does not appeal to me any more. It is not that much of a challenge. But sometimes I wish I had a little

more passion and I was a little less objective. A lot of times compromising is the worst thing you can do.

"In the old days some of the best things we did came because we'd work and work until we had just the right line, and it made the difference between something that was interesting and OK and something that really caught your attention."

Who knows what makes commercials sell? *Originality, jolt, impact,* every month there is a new buzz word in the ad business as another expert comes up with the explanation. But one implied comparison runs through such talk— the metaphor of war. An idea works like a grenade: a flash, a loud noise, and then the shrapnel slices deep into our brain. The best ideas catch us off guard; just when we expect a spokesman to praise, he jokes; just when we are going to sneer at a new-car introduction, the actor threatens to tear off a bumper. The tone is aggressive. The best moves surprise and conquer, like the strategy of a good general. Some commercials even work like an ambush: our mind gets caught in the emotional and intellectual crossfire between what we see and what we hear, between image and slogan. And, dazed in this electronic battlefield, we are described as "hooked," "knocked out," or "killed." What makes a winning general in this psychological war for the hearts and minds of the people? A certain toughness and looseness seem to help more than any specific style or craft. Call it a hard-hitting personality, if you will, or call it pizazz. As Sanford Haver, creative director for Colgate Palmolive advertising, says, "There are two things you need to write great commercials: temperament and talent. And 99 and 44/100ths of it is temperament."

overdirected

In primitive times Celtic kings hired sorcerers to cast a "glamour" over a hill to make the enemy imagine a fortress where there was only a hut. Nowadays the strategists of commercials seek such magical interference with our vision from a director. For approximately $2,000 a day a director is expected to add a glow to the idea. The director sets up bright-bright lights and brings wraparound lenses in for giant close-ups of superactive scenes, featuring realer than real consumers. The best directors hypo the hype.

Unlike a real movie director, the director of a commercial does not work with the writer during the process of writing; he is not consulted about the script before it is submitted to him for a bid; and often he does not meet the cast until the day of the shoot. He may not change the basic story, or the characters, during the shoot. And although he may have the right to try his own editing, he almost never controls the final version, since the ad agency steps in, choosing the shots they like and ordering those shots the way they like.

Because his control is cramped in so many important ways, a director of commercials has a limited range of decisions to make (lights, camera, acting, sets), but even in this restricted field a good director can make the difference between humdrum and startling appearance. Directors add gloss. Directors work in film, which still provides slightly sharper images, clearer depth of field, stronger colors than videotape; since most of the programs are made on videotape, because it is fast, cheap, and relatively easy to edit, these commercials *look* better than the shows. And individual directors do show their own taste in the composition of shots (Rick Levine, for instance, tends to shoot very head-on or at right angles), in lighting (Elbert Budin manages extraordinary glowing lights that seem to come from inside the Schmidt's beer, Sunkist oranges, or Breyer's Peach Ice Cream), camera focal length (Budin magnifies one grain of Uncle Ben's rice

until it seems almost six inches high on a large home set), and actors' moods (Mike Cuesta gets his Spanish-American actors to relax enough for some improvised dialogue, giving his *Graduation* spot the feeling of a documentary rather than a rehearsed play). Most directors have backgrounds in still photography and hate videotape; they love film and often imagine that they are imitating Howard Hawks, John Ford, or Frank Capra, the three personal idols they mention most. But, since they do not have control of script, location, cast, and editing, these directors do not enjoy the freewheeling, almost authorial control of a Hollywood pro.

So the personality of a director tends to show up in his choice of specialization. You might not think it, but each major product category has its conventions (wine ads are misty; shampoos require brilliantly back-lit showers), and some directors polish those conventions to a slick gleam. One director excels at food, another at cars; a third can handle animals and kids well; still another actually works with grown-up human actors to get a strong performance. (This is known as "people-directing.")

Tony Ficalora, for instance, shows us food the way it might appear to a baby rolling in it or to a starving man hallucinating in the desert. Ficalora can make a salad dressing seem like a waterfall and a salad like a jungle. In one spot we move through the lettuce leaves slowly—as moisture from above drips into the camera—nosing our way to the heart of the greenery. Only when red dressing slops down onto these giant bushes do we realize that our sense of scale has been fooled and we are actually in the bowl. In another spot for Kraft, giant eggs roll toward us, lumbering left and right, until one gets picked up and cracked at the end. That frame freezes motion in glistening light while the mayonnaise label appears.

Sometimes these epic foodstuffs are real, and sometimes Ficalora has them built, as when he constructed a giant tomato for a Sacramento tomato juice spot. Bob Warner, the production chief for that commercial, recalls that Ficalora built the tomato in sections in his brownstone and had it trucked to the studio. "The biggest problem was what to do with this tomato. For months afterward, Ficalora would call me and say, 'What do you want me to do with this tomato?' It was still lying around, and he couldn't just ignore it."

Ficalora might prefer taking pictures of people, but agencies hire him for spots in which we see hands and food rather than humans. The characters—when there are any—in his commercials rarely have spoken dialogue. When we see whole bodies, they are usually just moving rather than talking, as in the Rubbermaid spot

ANNOUNCER: Wedges of tasty Swiss . . . and ice-cold Fyfe & Drum Beer.

ANNOUNCER: Stir Crazy, the way to pop popcorn, made only by West Bend.

where the two garbagemen toss a Rubbermaid trash container under their slash bar and the Rubbermaid bounces back.

Ficalora likes vast banquets. His home economist (a director who works with food has to have one) knows how to cook for looks—and how to keep the food looking luscious despite hours under the hot lights. She will bake ten chocolate cakes, a dozen chickens, in succession, bringing each out of the oven at intervals so that there

will always be a fresh one in front of the camera. And in his best films, Mateus rosé comes surrounded with slippery hot lobsters and misty grapes; Celeste pizza drips oil and cheese as we lift a slice; another hand-size food becomes a basketball for Tropicana.

Such directorial exaggeration enlarges our appetite, encouraging us to dream of jumping into our food as if it were a pile of hay. When a Ficalora orange opens, so many giant drops of juice fly out in a medium-size TV that, if they were real, we could use up a whole sheet of Bounty cleaning the screen. Surreal? He seems medieval to me, like an archetype of the Glutton, whose eye is bigger than his belly.

Andy Jenkins, by contrast, likes to work outdoors, shooting supposed "locals" and "real people," making fake scenes seem more real than any hand-held documentary ever could. Follow-

WEST BEND Through video trickery, the lady walks below the popcorn poppers without getting buttered. (*left*)
FYFE & DRUM Extreme close-ups make food look as large as it did to us when we were small. (*above*)

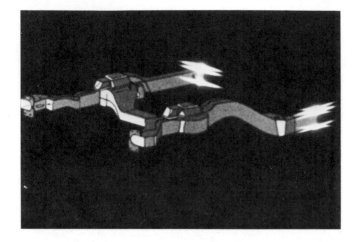

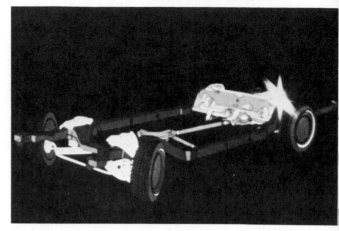

ing the maxim that seeing is believing, Jenkins persuades us by his attentive work with actors, generating whole lives for people who appear for only three seconds, and building a complete town or home for them, even if we see only one corner. Often these grizzled inhabitants are actors, but with Jenkins, they woof and scratch and go around looking like "jes folks." He set fire to an abandoned barn for Metropolitan Life. We see chickens run from an old-fashioned fire truck; we see geezers staring; we hear the grateful farmer hold out his thanks to the firemen— "You boys want a couple of chickens?" Except for the fact that every shot is gorgeous and full of active detail, we might think this brief film had been shot during a real fire. Jenkins' most spectacular spot shows the misty dunes of Kitty Hawk or Cape Hatteras; we see the tan plane clearly, it comes toward us, it takes off, then we soar with it, over the first hill of sand. The mood is gentle, lovely, gray. Jenkins likes intricate construction: he built the Wright Brothers' plane for that spot; and for Owens-Corning, he built an igloo in the Mojave desert and insulated it with their Fiberglas. It did not melt.

Bob Giraldi, a popular director, costs five to ten thousand dollars more than a nonstar direc-

GENERAL MOTORS   Computer-controlled   TV studies create a car out of lines of light.

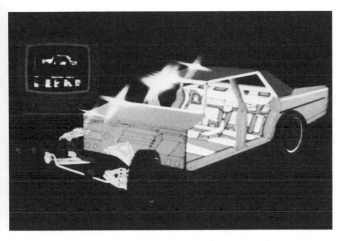

tor, but he can give you a dreamy "look" that will glamorize your product. He once did an antique spot for Barney's, showing how the men's store started; he used forty suits from the period and shot the whole in sepia; only when we come up to the present do we enter a world of color. Giraldi shot a karate dojo in yellowish light, showing slow-motion turns and kicks, then went to a bar for the after-workout drink of Miller's; the bar is darker, crowded with reds and browns, and the beer seems to light it up. Lots of smiles, daps, and handshakes here: so we get two spaces, two moods. For Arrow shirts he re-created an upper crust British garden party in such detail that a regular movie director would wince with envy; for Pioneer he made beautiful pictures of the interior of Carnegie Hall.

Giraldi started as a still photographer, and many of his notions of beauty stem from the conventional standards of excellence in still photography, at least those of the Sixties: lush detail, subtle range of colors, tricky angles. But he casts actors very well, and he understands the Stanislavski method; in theatrical terms, he can direct a cast, drawing out a real period performance from them. (Many commercial direc-

tors are content with a reading.) Like a Hollywood pro, he has a fondness for period sets, fancy film techniques, and mood pieces. Naturally Giraldi is what Bob Warner calls a strong director. He works hard, too, starting around 7:30 in the morning. But, he says, "We try to add fun and excitement to our job. When you work until midnight nearly every day, you need to have some fun."

Fun, for Giraldi, means brief bursts of beauty —but even he usually leaves editing to the agency. One of the few directors who does keep the kind of total control a Hollywood pro does is Dan Nichols, and he started out as a writer. He was creative director of the McDonald's account for Needham, Harper & Steers when they decided that the old song "You Deserve a Break Today" had become shopworn. He and his boss spent two weeks out of phone contact with the rest of the world, locked in the Drake Hotel. They came up with a dozen different campaign ideas, each with its own song. There was one that everyone at the ad agency loved. Everyone hated "You, you're the one." But Nichols liked it. "The reason I was in love with it was that it was so simplistic, it was so blatantly directed at the consumer."

Nichols' involvement with the writing allows him to plan the high volume of scenes in his spots; in one sixty-second McDonald's spot he showed sixty-five scenes, and in most spots he crams in fast cuts, zooms, and reverses. For one commercial about McDonald's take-out food, called *Ice Nine,* he figured out sixty-four potential snow scenes and listed them in categories; under "Downhill Skiing," for instance, he listed these shots:

1) Aerials of skis, flip, spread eagles, layouts, crossing
2) Ski race start at timing gate
3) High-speed powder skiing
4) High-speed slalom
5) Mogul head bops
6) Kite
7) Ski jump (high speed)
8) 36-degree pole swings
9) Cross-country skiing
10) Hot dogging . . . ballet

After that ten seconds, we go on to look at ice skating, snow chores, sledding, snow romps, snow school, snow sports, picnickers in the snow eating McDonald's take-out food, and girls indoors, "nice and warm."

One McDonald's spot is titled *Quick Cuts,* and that is Nichols' style. To be seen and recognized in half a second, each scene must be clear, well-lit, and carefully planned. If we pan left in one scene, we often pan right in the next; if we are moving forward for one second, we may pull back in the next. His editing establishes a rhythm of movement: two stills, a move forward, a move back, a still, then the camera holds still while someone moves past it to the right, then back to the left. He uses frozen frames like dotted notes, or syncopation, holding one image for a while so that the next one is more sharply emphasized. They mark the end of one sequence of ski sports, the beginning of ice hockey scenes; they give us a rest. In another one, each frozen frame shows us a person, the target of the song

"You, you're the one." Nichols comments, "My formula is energy. You have to keep it going."

Such complex, baroque visions make McDonald's seem dense with life—lots of physical movement, lots of memorable snapshots. But ultimately such spots are as artificial as a McDonald's shake. Perhaps that very artificiality—the "madeness" of the spots—appeals to Americans at least as much as the whetted-up vitality. There are two men who disagree: David and Albert Maysles believe people want to look at reality, and they have made grimy documentary films like *Grey Gardens,* focusing on two aging and slightly batty relatives of Jacqueline Onassis, *Gimme Shelter,* in which the Hell's Angels stomp people at the Rolling Stones' concert in Altamont, and *Salesman,* in which they trail Bible salesmen around the country. Their films seem unrehearsed. As David Maysles says, "The viewer never really knows what's coming up next because that's the way it was shot. The photographer doesn't know what's coming up next." When they make a film, they pay for it themselves, so they keep complete control. But they pay for these feature films by making spots.

They do not charge the advertiser much because they just take their cameras out on location and talk to real people who use the product or make it. "The transition from documentaries to commercials wasn't as difficult as you'd think," says David Maysles. "The copywriters and art directors did most of the research in picking the people we were going to work with, and then we shot as we normally do." Bob Judd and Jerry Weldor of J. Walter Thompson located a Champion Spark Plug dealer who would let them film him; we see him chat with customers, go out to service a broken-down car, wave at the camera. He seems friendly, at ease. Evidently it took a few hours for him to relax, but after a while he just went ahead with his work without "acting" and the results seem casual and comfortable. Nothing hard-hitting, but something fairly intimate. Then there's the spot they did for IBM in which we see one employee after another wishing us Happy New Year—it's moving because there are so many and they seem to be having such a good time with the cameraman. Advertising coffee, the Maysles shot an impromptu basketball game in a gym; as guys came off the court to relax, they were asked if they had drunk coffee for breakfast. Yes, indeed. It looks like luck, but a lot of the casual, friendly mood comes from the down-home directness of the men behind the camera.

Reality, then, is a certain "look." "You've got to give the Maysles their head, or you shouldn't hire them," says Howard Rieger of Young & Rubicam. That could apply to any of these top directors. But the Maysles lived with one family for three days just to get a picture of them eating Jell-O. "For Jell-O we wanted spontaneous, natural, believable dialogue," says Rieger. "If you're looking for reality, they're the guys."

Perhaps. But once "reality" is sliced into a commercial selling a dream of coffee as a high-energy food, we reenter the fantasy realm. Perhaps, as Aristotle suggested, we want to believe in dramas and get angry only when forced to face their open falsity. So a high premium gets put on making the lie believable, shiny, hypnotic, luscious, active, and arresting. In a commercial, it seems, the director is the person who makes the genuinely artificial food substitute look more deliciously real than steak. And Americans love it—we eat dreams.

o make their magic more hypnotic, to snare and entrance our dreaming mind by giving it a central figure to focus on, admen put stars in their commercials. These stars are often malleable, like the figures in erotic daydreams. Semiknown actors—who can stand for any number of values and emotions—often work better than those who have developed a consistent character; John Wayne, for instance, could not convince anyone he ever got a headache, so no one could imagine him using Datril. His commercials for this product lacked credibility. If we recognize a face but cannot quite figure out where we saw it before, we are free to assume that this is a hero, and from there on we are free to follow the sponsor's suggestions while imagining his character any way we please. Animals make even better stars—they're cute and unthreatening, so we treat them like babies, or pets. Who could imagine one of them tricking us into buying something? But they do—their appeal is transferred to the product, and we often end up paying for it in the store.

Putting one actor or actress in the neon halo, commercials perpetuate the star system and, in some cases, actually provide us with new folk heroes, new national pets. Who's the hero? At Wells, Rich, Greene, they boast that their advertising makes the product the hero. They put a muffler in a golden light for almost half the length of some Midas commercials; and they show Bic cigarette lighters lighting people's cigarettes in one vignette after another. Parkay features spots in which the tub of margarine speaks to various users. And, speaking for Pontiac, Christine Meyers says, "We're making the cars the heroes. There are no excessive backgrounds. The cars are up front in all their naked beauty." No naked starlets, no humans evidently, just automobiles.

Sometimes the star is a member of the family next door—just folks. Ford found a family out in Texas to talk up its trucks. A teenager gets into a truck by a white fence; the logo reads, Clay Rightmer, 17 years old. He says, "My Daddy turned me onto Ford." Now Harold Rightmer, 42 years old, according to the logo, leans on the fence with a dog at his feet, and a herd of cattle behind him: "My Daddy said he always got good deals on cars and trucks from his Ford dealer." Now an older man, Charles Rightmer, shuffles along leading a horse: "My Daddy says if you own a 3,000-acre ranch, you need a tough truck, and your Ford dealer's got it." Will Rightmer, sitting down in front of an ancient Ford, says, "My Daddy came from Tennessee in a covered wagon. I had to learn about Fords on my own. I've been driving Fords most of my life." These down-home people probably sell the idea of Ford dependability better than half a dozen slicker actors could.

But most commercials focus on a central human being, played by a performer whose personality can make a mediocre idea seem funny or surprising. These actors (who are called "the talent") have to get paid, and even the lowest union fees can make an advertiser trim the cast, so the focus tends to zoom in on one or two people. Last year $100 million was paid to talent. Two unions represent principal players, those actors who actually speak on-camera as they stand in the foreground performing the service or reacting to the message. Extras, who get $155 for each day of shooting—and that's it—may cough in a crowd or watch in the background, but they are not principals, so they never get to tap residual payments. Residuals come to the principals, who get $218 a day these days, plus a complicated sliding scale for each time the commercial goes on the air. The agency has to pay a holding fee to each principal, too, just to maintain the right to air the commercial for the next thirteen weeks; if the commercial will go on the air in

---

ALFA ROMEO The car is the star. No other model dares to enter the ring.

the ten largest cities in the U.S., he may get $652.50. If the commercial will be used on a network, or in more than twenty shows, each actor gets $218.20 for the first use; $95 for the next; and $75 for the third through the thirteenth week. All told, some actors can earn fifteen thousand bucks in three months, even if you hardly know their names.

In fact, familiar-looking unknowns are favored as the central figures in many commercials, not just because they are cheaper than big names, but because they do not outshine the product. When John Wayne advertised that headache cure, we watched him, not the pill. Better are the popular spots for Lite Beer from Miller, which feature so many half-known sports figures that Miller had a contest to see which viewers could identify them all. One is Marvelous Marv Thornberry, a klutz for the Mets, who stands at a bar worrying that if he pitches their beer, Miller may lose money. Billy Martin, the combative manager of the Yankees, argues that he never argues; Bubba Smith tears the top off a can with his bare hands to show us how easy Lite Beer is to get at. Bob Lenz, Bob Engel, and Charles Ryant worked up fairly tight scripts at Miller's advertising agency, McCann Erickson, tested each jock out in black and white, then, if he looked okay, brought him to New York and got

him relaxed before shooting. Athletes are not professional actors, so they cannot be expected to go through the same spiel thirty times; but they are used to giving their best.

John de Butts is another of those people no one recognized until he went on TV; he replaced basketball star Bill Russell as spokesman for AT&T. De Butts is paid $484,000 a year as AT&T chairman, but he only got four glasses as payment for the spots; now he is recognized by taxi drivers, he says. Of course, former Olympic skier Suzy Chaffee has been plugging Chap Stick so much this season that even strangers call her Suzy Chapstick.

Such semipros come without the gloss of Hollywood, so they deflect the cynicism we feel about actors—that they are "just acting."

Ball players top the list of non-actorish spokesmen. They offer a tough, strong look—the model of male authority in our still-macho culture. They often seem too innocent, or too dumb, to lie. And they lend an animal energy and charm to perfectly unathletic products. As soon as Reggie Jackson clinched the world championship for the Yankees in 1977, his price per commercial jumped from $25,000 to $35,000, and his agent, Lloyd Kolmer, announced, "He gets top dollar." The day after the Series ended, Kolmer got calls from a bank, a ham, and an after-shave;

ANNOUNCER: In this corner Alfetta by Alfa Romeo, four-time World Champion.

In this corner . . . nobody.

POP: Neighbor, how long has it been since you had a big, thick, steaming bowl of Wolf Brand Chili? (CHUCKLES) Well, that's too long!

they wanted him fast because he was instantly recognizable, and Kolmer wanted to make deals before everyone forgot. Within a month Puma athletic shoes, Rawlings Sporting Goods baseball gloves, and Fabergé were signed, and Standard Brands is now bringing out a new candy bar called The Reggie Bar. Reggie's manager appears in another spot with some giant feet which he sprays with MP 27: "Sure glad he's not an umpire." And former catcher and now manager Yogi Berra plugs Jockey T Shirts in a funny spot with his kids; he comes out for short hair and white underwear; they choose long hair and color. At the end he appeals to us: "Where did I go wrong?" O. J. Simpson has run through airports so much for Hertz that Avis made a new spot saying, "You don't have to run through airports if you sign up with us."

And ex-slugger Joe DiMaggio made Mr. Coffee the best-selling automatic coffee-brewer in the country through his simple but sympathetic pitch. He gets $100,000 a year for that—but, he says, "I probably would not have had anything to do with the product if I didn't own it." He won the coffee-maker in a golf tournament. Now Sophia Loren plugs water for Mr. Coffee under an arrangement between Lloyd Kolmer and the

coffee-maker's manufacturer. For twenty seconds she sells Mr. Coffee; then she turns and points out their water filter system, called Filter Fresh. "We want the visibility," says Darrol Solin at Ted Bates. "And she's highly credible, speaks very well, has done cookbooks, and she's known as a housewife and a mother as well." Evidently the Ted Bates people didn't know she's sometimes known as a film star as well.

Helen Van Slyke, who retired as creative vice president at Norman Craig and Kummel to write six best-selling novels, including *Always Is Not Forever*, argues that using a star can only work if he's advertising something we would expect him to know about. "Why on earth should I bank where Joe DiMaggio tells me to? Just because he's rich? He's an ex-ballplayer, not a financial genius, as far as I know. Andy Griffith does not motivate me to buy crackers, or Angie Dickinson vermouth. I don't believe they care about those things any more than I think Duke Wayne ever has a headache, even though he's touting its remedy.

"On the other side of the coin, I would buy Donald O'Connor's remedy for athlete's foot (though I deplore the commercial) or try a perfume recommended by Catherine Deneuve, or lust for a mink when I see Diana Vreeland wearing one in an ad. I mean, they're selling me something I think they know something about. I only wish a burglar alarm system would sign Angie, or a blue jeans company take on Andy." Unfortunately, tests show that Bugs Bunny moves more products than Catherine Deneuve, even if it ain't carrots. Audiences, it seems, are not as logical as Ms. Van Slyke, and Lord Olivier makes Polaroid seem like high art, Billie Jean King makes Carnation Instant Breakfast look healthy. Eleanor Roosevelt may have started the celebrity plug when she did a spot for margarine; paid $35,000, she bought a lot of CARE packages for starving children, but she also set off an onslaught of testimonials from people like Ricardo

Montalban (Chrysler Cordoba), Robert Morley (BOAC), Muhammad Ali (his own Rope-a-Dope), Johnny Cash (Lionel Trains), Florence Henderson (Wessonality), and Bob Hope (Texaco). Jackie Gleason now competes with a six-inch-high puppet, the Pillsbury Dough Boy, as spokesman for cake mixes; Gleason is just as chubby, but he costs more. Leo Burnett persuaded him to do test commercials for less than $200,000, but agent Lloyd Kolmer suspects Gleason will get even more if the campaign goes national. "He was one of the big star holdouts," says Marty Ingels, another talent agent. "We've asked him before, and he didn't need the money."

Giant stars from sports or entertainment bring their own followers to the product, particularly if we can believe they might actually use the product at home; for a sponsor, such performers are well worth their high cost. If we already like to daydream about Ali or Reggie, the commercials help us by showing the hero in a new scene, with a new product. And if we want to bring the dream closer to reality, we can buy and eat that product, too.

Some stars are aware of this power and advertise to sponsors that they are available. Howdy Doody and his pal Buffalo Bob used to plug Tootsie Rolls, Hostess Twinkies, Wonder bread, and Colgate toothpaste on the old *Howdy Doody Show;* now Bob's agent, Jack Drury, thinks the pair should be hired again to work on those kiddies who have grown up. "Today," he points out in an ad in *Advertising Age,* "those very children of the nationwide Peanut Gallery are young adults with families of their own, careers, bank accounts, cars, homes and television sets. They are the very market that most advertisers long to reach." So far no one has taken him up on that. But his argument is valid. Stars bring their own audiences into the commercial, lend credibility built up in mythic roles on screen or sports fields, and they do transfer some portion

PELE (IN PORTUGUESE): Do you know me?

of that magic to the product. So if you have a new product that no one will believe in, or a service in a field most people mistrust, a star can persuade people to give you a try. Twenty-three percent of those commercials rated as the 100 Best in *Advertising Age*'s annual competition come with big stars, most of whom haul down huge salaries—Sir Laurence Olivier, $500,000 from Polaroid; Henry Fonda, $275,000 a year from GAF; Kirk Douglas, $150,000 a year from Bulova.

Clearly, animals would be cheaper. Cats and dogs come at $25 an hour, but if you're pushing pet food, you have to persuade them to eat *your* brand. (To give them anything else is considered deceptive advertising.) Other animals are more expensive: lions cost $150 an hour, and elephants $600 plus trucking. But even if one of these animals eats your extras, or stomps your

WOLF CHILI This friendly local sheriff reminds his neighbors that even though statistics show they buy Wolf Chili, they should use it more often so they can buy more. (*opposite*)

AMERICAN EXPRESS Playing on the fact that we forget famous faces fast, American Express points out that even though you may be important in your own arena, other people may not recognize you; therefore, you need a card to give you credit. (*above*)

set, you don't have to pay residuals. So there are scores of commercials that make animals their stars. Cunningham & Walsh wanted to symbolize the kind of person who never uses the Yellow Pages; how about an ostrich? someone said. So they wrote the spot that way. Then someone called the Bronx Zoo to ask them how to get an ostrich to stick its head in the sand. The zoo keeper said, "They never do that." And indeed they don't. So the humans dig a hole, put a man in the hole holding the ostrich's head under the sand, and then they let the ostrich pull its head out. They ran that film backwards so it looked like the ostrich was actually putting his head in the sand. The zoo keeper saw this on the air, and called up in amazement: "How did you get him to put his head in the sand?"

Animals can become almost a trademark, a signature, as one Cunningham & Walsh writer, Joe Brown, found out when he was doing commercials for Qantas. "When we got the account, no one knew what Qantas was. It's not a name of something; it's an acronym. Queensland Auckland National Transportation and so forth. It was a very fine airline, but it had a lot of competition from giants. And they obviously didn't have the money to put behind a campaign for that airline that would generate the recognition that Pan Am has as a competitor. So we wanted an advertising idea that would break through for very little money, relatively speaking. And the koala bear as a signature turned out to be one of the most successful ways you can do this. A smaller-budget advertiser can make some noise and can develop a sales pattern. And sales dramatically improved. I think they're number one on that route. That's among the top ten devices that have been recorded. You know, we never show airplanes in these airline ads." Instead we see beefy men rushing surfboards and boats into the waves. And up on the beach, speaking, is a koala bear. "And who flies those tourists to sightsee me? Qantas, that's who. . . . I hate Qantas."

On stationery, fire helmets, silver medallions, and recently TV spots, the Hartford Insurance Group has used a stag as its image. The director of advertising, Leonard Watson, worried about putting the stag on TV: "I had many second thoughts. I was worried that the stag would overpower the message, or would look ridiculous and undignified." But he swallowed his scruples and Hartford sent the stag out to the West Coast—where the commercial would be filmed —in a four-horse trailer, the only vehicle that could accommodate the stag's rack of antlers. "For the first time in the history of television advertising," Watson boasts, "a company has been made symbolically present as the major character in its commercials in a way that is neither childish nor surreal." The appeal, though, is to the child in us: here is Bambi's Daddy. Rugged, alert, strong, the stag looks in on the people insured by the Hartford, watching over a pet shop, peering through a sheet of plate glass at a big factory (where they are making stained-glass pictures of him, naturally), gazing at a helicopter lifting off with a load of cargo at the airport. He keeps an eye on truckers as part of the Hartford antihijacking program. And he noses a tricycle off the sidewalk to avoid acci-

Courtesy of Lever Brothers Co.

STEVE PLAYS A FEW NOTES.
EYDIE: You know, Steve, no matter how
many times we sing on TV, I never got
used to that camera.

STEVE: I know what you mean, Eydie. It
sees everything.

dents around the home. Earl Hammond, the stag's trainer, had grown up on his father's elk farm in Nebraska, so he knew how to teach the deer to walk up stairs, look in windows, and stare at cars. The secret? He hid Oreo and Tollhouse cookies, plus apples and corn, in the right spots, and the deer went from spot to spot to get his treats. On location one time the deer was not lifting his head up to suit the director, Dick Cunha, so he started yelling at the deer with an electric bullhorn. The copywriter tried mooing. Finally they brought in an eight-year-old lion to attract the deer's attention. The lion didn't faze the deer: instead, he started eating the trees on the set. The prop men sprayed the leaves with Lysol to stop him, but the deer liked Lysol and kept on eating. What with Lysol, trees, and Oreos, the stag got a full belly fast, and so he could only work twice a week. Even so, ten thousand feet of film was shot, enough to make the ninety feet used in the sixty-second spot.

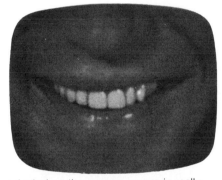

And when the camera comes in really
close . . . that's when our teeth just
have to be their whitest.

PEPSODENT Worried about the way their teeth look close up, Steve and Eydie interrupt a recording session to talk about toothpaste.

EYDIE: That's why Pepsodent's our
toothpaste.

I'm left speechless.

QANTAS The koala bear plugs the Australian airline by complaining about how many tourists they bring onto his beaches. Here he squats and comments sourly on the arriving planes, and tests out the champagne served on the flights. (*above and opposite*)

NATIONAL CAR Don Rickles stars as the world's toughest critic, checking out the rental car with sarcasm and grumbling while the clerks smile and help him out. After one year of these spots, 45% more people were aware of National Car Rental than before. (*left*)

Because they spotlight the central figure so well—whether it is animal, vegetable, or mineral—commercials sometimes attract new audiences for the performers. When this happens, we see how much audiences and producers want new stars; they're even willing to pluck them out of a commercial. Thus, by following the conventions established by our national daydreams, commercials do not just use stars; they create them. In 1971 Sandy Duncan played a United California Bank teller trying hard to pronounce the name of a customer, Nicholas Janopopropolus, while the announcer claimed that UCB had the best tellers in town or your money back. She won half a dozen awards in commercial circles, got named Woman of the Year by the Hollywood radio and TV society, and went on to two TV series and movies. She said afterward, "Commercials are a great training ground for young actors. . . . I ought to know. Even though I had some small success on Broadway, it took New York filmed commercials for the United California Bank to really put my film and TV career into high gear."

One man who never thought about a show business career got one anyway, thanks to some commercials he did for Old Home Bread. Bill Fries was working for Bozell & Jacobs in Omaha when he wrote a spot called "Nice Buns." We would hear a trucker talking in time to a rough rhythm, talking blues style, about his life carrying around Old Home Bread. Here is a sample:

Well . . . Interstate Eighty, Ah's cookin' a-live . . .
    thermometer read about a hundred an' five.
Had a ten-ton Old Home Bread truck a humpin' all
    day,
    Pumpin' out steam!
Had a thousand cubes . . . an' they was runnin' cool . . .

HARTFORD INSURANCE GROUP   This stag keeps watch over you, just like an insurance agent. But during the filming he sometimes stared the wrong way, forcing the crew to shout and hoot.

was till ah run outa bread-truck fuel
at th' Old Home filler up n' keep on a truckin' ca–fe.
Gimme ten gallon. Well,
    She filled m'tank . . . ah said Thank ya honey . . .
    Name was Mavis . . . Ah gave 'er the money . . .
    sez howabout an Old Home Burger an'
    ice cream cone . . . to cool myself off with.
Putta patty on th' grill 'n back she came . . . sez
    tell me truck-man what's yer name? Ah said
    C. W. McCall 'n ah haul for Old Home. You can
    call m' C. W.
Well, ah give 'er a wink 'n she eye-balled me . . .
    it was Old Home luv plain t' see.
Then she handed me an Old Home Burger on a
    purty pink tray.
    A nice fresh bun.
Well, ah finished up the burger . . . said bye-now Hon.
An then ah left 'er a truck-load 'a Old Home buns . . .
fer th' Old Home filler up n' keep on a truckin' cafe.
Old Home is Good Buns!

Fries says, "It was not a big account, and we were looking around for a voice, you know? I didn't have much budget, and I couldn't find the right guy. I wanted something dry, and everyone was overacting. I made the demo to show people what I wanted. People back at the agency heard that tape and said, 'Why don't you do it?' It would save money, they figured." So he recorded the voice-over as a low-key song. Then people started asking for copies of the song. The agency put out a record, and it caught on. Soon MGM Records (now known as Polydore) signed him up—they wanted a whole album, so Fries worked one up, drawing on personal experience. He wrote a trucking song that went to the top of the country and western charts and another song called "Black Bear Mountain," about four-wheel-drive jeeping on hairy roads. "Convoy," a song about truckers and their CB radios, was *Variety*'s Number One seller for seven straight weeks and then, according to Fries, it "crossed over, got to the top of the pop charts. On New Year's Day, 1976, it was Number One in the country. It was the most requested song in the history of most stations. We sold five million." He was a star.

Fries liked being a music-maker, but the star trip—the obligatory round of concerts and personal appearances—exhausted him. He quit his job at the ad agency, retired from the concert circuit, and holed up in a cabin 8,000 feet up in the Colorado Rockies with his family.

Commercials that use and abuse their central figures mirror our national need for stars—first for Mom, then for athletic men, gonzo truckers, and appealing bank tellers, and finally for lovable furry animals. And the commercials are designed to make us identify our unconscious fantasies of the powerful Mom or Dad, or the weak but cute baby we think we used to be with those high-glow dreams flashing in front of us. We recognize our inner life being played out with a product.

In Greek tragedy the moment of recognition, called anagnorisis, often came through tokens, as when the long-lost son recognizes that the woman in front of him has on a necklace with the missing fragment of his own amulet and thinks, "Why, this must be my mother!" In America commercials are the dramas we see over and over—our brief classics. And once we are caught up in them, imagining ourselves the hero, or the person he saves, we tend to invest that psychic energy in the box he holds in his hand, or the car he drives. The product, then, becomes a trigger to memory, and when we see it in storefront or showroom, we can find ourselves replaying the whole thirty-second fantasy, replacing an unknown actor with our own face, or cozying up to the superstar by one act: purchase.

Buy the token, and you get an instant replay of your electronic daydream. As Aristotle said when writing about Greek drama, the best recognition scenes involve the hero discovering something about his own nature rather than his bracelet. But Americans, in general, prefer and pay for stars who understand themselves in terms of products—token stars.

ITT A trip to Europe, thousands of small yellow sticks, and a near massacre made producing this commercial an unexpected extravagance.

One measure of the energy admen put into making dreams look real is the money spent on production. Simply staging and filming a thirty-second spot in which an announcer just stands there holding a product can cost over $20,000 when you include labor, editing, and duplicating the final commercial to send around to TV stations. But people tend to tune out mere talking heads, so writers search for the exotic location, the wild break-apart car, the overdone dramatic scene, the coloratura graphics. These can drive costs up to $60,000 at 1978 prices, and if you add a kickline, as in the Busby Berkeley dance-hall routine done for Heinz' "great American soups," you may find production costs alone running over a quarter of a million dollars. If you were to make a feature film at the same rate per second, you would have to pay thirty million.

It is a strange fantasy world that is reflected in these seconds-long extravaganzas. We see ourselves dancing in a pinball machine, chopping down trees in forests we have never visited; the impossible seems as likely in this world as a car driving down a canal. A paranoid's worst fears are acted out by tanks running over his foot, or a plane landing on his rug; we can follow our unconscious impulses even if it means leaving the football parade to run home for another bite of Kellogg's Raisin Bran. We see miraculous transformations—people whose bodies suddenly bloat up or turn into bright outlines—we can imagine we have the power to hurl a car into space. We can fantasize about impressing a billionaire. More than any show on adult TV, commercials put their money on the unconscious, reshooting, tinkering, editing, perfecting the unreal until it almost seems real, making

extravagantly produced

ANNOUNCER: We deliberately sent this car skidding out of control to illustrate what causes most skidding accidents . . . wheels that lock on a slippery road.

one image turn into another at the sound of some disembodied voice, as in our interior life. Admen, sponsors, and audiences participate in these expensive fantasies. Perhaps such productions work for us because they approach the clarity, force, and speed of dreams.

But this dreamworld costs money, at least if we want to see it with Kodak detail on TV. The producer, in fact, has to act like a foreman for God, bossing around forty or fifty people, building the sets, soothing the director, terrifying the talent. He must create—and destroy—a small universe in less than a week. In the Fifties a producer really did run the whole show, but gradually his role has been reduced from that of a lofty archangel to that of an officious angel with the spirit of an accountant. In the Fifties and early Sixties a producer working for J. Walter Thompson or some other advertising agency would call up three or four production houses and say, "I've finally got a script here; we'd like you to bid on it." The production house would look at the outline of the commercial, figure on yellow paper, and call back with a total dollar figure; for that money, the agency would get 4,500 feet of clear, professionally shot film, ready to be edited. But big spenders like Lever Brothers or Procter & Gamble wanted to know exactly where their pennies were going, so they made up forms which the production houses had to fill out, showing the budget breakdown. In the late Sixties, after years of dickering, the Association of Independent Commercial Producers—the production houses—made up their own forms so that their people could fill out the same slots, no matter what agency or sponsor they were dealing with. Here is a list of some of the costs a producer has to figure:

PREPRODUCTION AND POST-PRODUCTION COSTS
SHOOTING CREW LABOR
STUDIO COSTS: BUILDING SET, SHOOTING TIME, STRIKING SET
TRAVEL TO, EXPENSES AT, LOCATION

This 7¼" Black & Decker circular saw can work, and work,

EQUIPMENT COSTS
FILM STOCK
PROPS, COSTUMES, ANIMALS
PAYROLL TAXES
DIRECTOR'S FEE
INSURANCE
MARKUP FOR PRODUCER
EDITING
EXTRA DAYS IF BAD WEATHER STRIKES
CAMERA OPERATOR
PROP CREW
ELECTRICIANS
GRIPS
RECORDING MAN
BOOM MAN
MAKEUP
HAIR STYLIST
WARDROBE STYLIST
HOME ECONOMIST
VIDEO ENGINEER
NURSE
GENERATOR MAN
ACTORS
STUNTMAN
STILL PHOTOGRAPHER
LOCATION SCOUT
TEAMSTERS

Five pages break these items down even further, and one page summarizes the costs. Most commercials in 1978 run from $20,000 to $40,000 to make, but fancy ones regularly go up to

and work,

really hard. When America has a job to do, it reaches for Black & Decker.

$60,000 and $100,000, and exceptional ones can run past $250,000, plus deposits of as much as $1,000,000 as insurance against damage. The cash register starts ringing as soon as you decide to use animals or kids (they are unpredictable, hard to work with, slow, and fussy, so they add days to the shooting time), to go on location in lousy weather (rain postpones shooting a day, but everyone has to sit there in the tent getting paid), to do it in a rush (you may have to use videotape—with a lot of generators, ticklish gear, and temperamental color cameras—just because with videotape you can edit as soon as you have gotten a shot you like, and you can then go on the air that night instead of waiting for film developing and editing, which takes days and sometimes weeks), to try for special effects (you may have to take a few weeks to build a giant tomato, or you may have to buy time in a computer animation studio).

Most producers pad these bids so that if something goes wrong, they can absorb the cost overrun. If you have written about a herd of bulls galloping along the Mississippi next to a steamboat, as in one Merrill Lynch commercial, you will find that no one knows how much it costs to pay for run-amok bulls, frightened passersby, dung left on the pier, and drowned cattle. So

most production houses add a hundred thousand dollars to the estimate, just to cover possibilities. Many big advertisers agree to pay all direct costs, giving the production house a certain percentage of those costs as its profit, and to make sure the production house does not simply run up the costs on the sly, the advertiser often has its own overseers who make sure that every penny spent is necessary. Poor folk, who only spend a few million a year on TV, cannot hire pros to go over the details, so they have to settle for a guaranteed bid: the production house says, in effect, "For $40,000 you get your commercial filmed; if we can keep costs down, we get the profit, but if costs run over that, we'll absorb the loss."

Most scriptwriters, of course, have no sense of costs. One who does is George Lois. "The production of my commercials is a piece of theatrics —but it's done very simply, with great strength. I'll shoot all six of these commercials in one day. It'll come out to maybe $4,000 on each one. Young & Rubicam, BBD&O, these cinematographers, these filmmakers, they run sixty, seventy, eighty, maybe a hundred thou a spot."

BLACK & DECKER   Want to saw down your barn? Here's how.

As Lois suggests, he is an exception. Many writers and ad directors tend to think big. Even if the commercial could be shot in a studio in New York or Los Angeles, as most are, writers tend to ignore how long it takes to capture just the right angle, the right smile, the exact exit. Time—with the entire crew waiting and getting paid to wait—costs the most. If you had a month to shoot, and if you could hire electricians and actors for an hour here and an hour there, you could spend much less. But admen are always late, and no one works for less than a full day, so a producer picks two days next month, hires everyone to come then, and the waiting begins.

Jerry Della Femina likes to write but hates to go on shoots. How come? He rolls his eyes to heaven. "Shooting? Shooting? Everybody be there at seven o'clock. You wonder why you must be there at seven o'clock. But you show up at seven o'clock. And you're there at seven o'clock watching guys move a camera. And we've improved everything in the world except the equipment you use to make a commercial. I mean, you pull and you push. There are two guys carrying things on their back, like over the Burma Road, guys stripped to the waist moving giant equipment over the floor, guys hurting themselves, breaking their backs. We shoot a commercial the way we used to build pyramids.

"Then there's the guy who stands there to spray food and make it look pretty. There's the guy who's assigned to read the *Daily News*. He

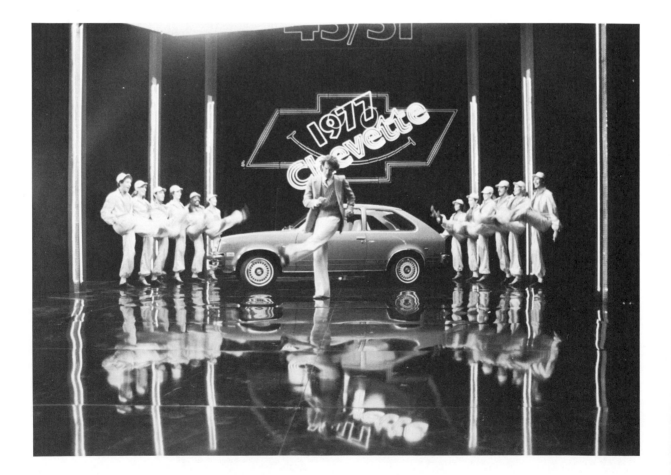

Reprinted by permission of American Motors, Inc.

CHEVROLET   Chevette stars in a Broadway musical. Will it kick off its wheels and dance? (*opposite*)

AMERICAN MOTORS   Riding on two wheels, apparently, the front half of a Pacer appears; then, seemingly without a driver, the rear half catches up. Secret: a hidden third wheel, and a midget driver in the back. (*above*) weighs two hundred and seventy-five pounds. You don't even want to ask him what else he does, because you know he's going to punch you. So he sits there. He never gets up. He never takes his eyes off that one column. And he's not sleeping. There's another guy who's sleeping. There are maybe thirty-five or forty guys running around doing things. There's the script-girl-timer-lady. Her main job is to look as though she can be made. She works hard. She's like the Red Cross lady, giving people donuts filled with garbage and bad coffee. Everyone's staring at the girl; at the beginning of the spot, the actors are playing to her. She's about thirty-one years old, attractive. She always has a stop watch in her hand. I always suspect that if she really went to bed with anyone, she'd be timing it. 'I'm sorry, that was twenty-seven seconds, you've got to try again.'

"And the first take is always at eleven thirty-five. Guy says, 'What do you think?' The director says, 'I think we should really set that up a little differently.' They set it up till about twelve-fifteen. Guy says, 'We got to break for lunch.' They always go to a very bad restaurant, somewhere downtown. They come back at two. They get their first shot.

"Now the time passes. The guy is still reading his *Daily News*. You look up, and it's eleven-thirty at night, and the director is getting very mad at everybody. The script girl will not go home with anybody. The actors are blowing their lines now; it's two in the morning, and everyone feels like they're in movies, they're Frank Capra or Harry Warner. If we were really in advertising, the shoot would be over at two o'clock in the afternoon. We'd get set up, shoot, get it done, pack, and get out. It would be fine. But everyone's getting ready for that great script, so we stay up until five in the morning."

At E.U.E. Productions, one of the few old-style production houses still functioning (most new production houses are really run by a single director, whereas E.U.E. still owns a stable of directors), I watched Fred Levenson direct a commercial for St. Regis Paper Company, plugging the corporation's high technology: it showed their protective masking material saving the day for a director of a Broadway musical. The material protects the tops of expensive rented pianos from damage when the chorus girls tap dance on them. (In real life, the polyethylene film protects the wings of aircraft from scratches when crews walk on them during refueling.) The producer, relieved to see he won't have to pay for any damage, lights up a cigar, and everyone thanks St. Regis. The morning the shoot is scheduled to begin, I ride up in the elevator with a red—well, henna-haired—woman who has got her garish locks done up in fifty curls and pins. She is wearing a plunging white gown, showing generous breasts, and she is carrying three very fake-jewel combs plus a Styrofoam cup of coffee-with-everything. Her name is Char Fontane, and she has played the lead in *Grease* on Broadway; she speaks fluent Italian, sings, dances, and acts for Ivory, Pampers, and Coke. Today she's going to play "The Producer's Girl Friend."

We come through narrow beige corridors, doubling back past conference rooms, bulletin boards covered with call lists, labs. We step through the safety door, and find black drapes hanging from the twenty-foot ceiling to the snakepit of cables on the floor. "Ken, get me a glass of cold water," someone says through a gap.

Stafford Ordahl, the copy supervisor from Cunningham & Walsh, meets me and shows me through the drapes. "It's a bigger deal than the bullfight," he comments, recalling the commercial he had made earlier for St. Regis in which a bull charges at the camera, only to be deflected by St. Regis's clear plastic sheeting. I count forty-nine people here, a dozen of whom seem to be executives from St. Regis with their wives. I end up standing next to a seventeen-foot-high red

CHEVROLET PICKUP TRUCKS ARE EQUIPPED WITH
GM-BUILT ENGINES PRODUCED BY VARIOUS DIVISIONS
SEE YOUR DEALER FOR DETAILS.

hydraulic jack; on top of it, a light that is three feet in diameter heats up the set.

"What's that?" asks another visitor, sweating in a black suit, pointing at two yard-square panels of black metal with a billy club handle.

"That's a rheostat," says one of the stage crew.

"Jay, we'll move up with you, 'cause this is going to get a little hot."

He's right. I take off my sweater. In front of me is a row of twenty-four 500-watt spots lighting the stage from the dusty floor. The rear wall is mirrored, and a man stands on a ladder there, spraying the mirror with window cleaner, wiping it, over and over. Right in front of me, aiming his camera over the footlights at the pianos and their reflections, the director, Fred Levenson, signals he is ready. He calls to an actor by one piano, "Tony, come closer to the piano as you're walking around it, OK?"

Tony Travis nods. He is a veteran of over 100 spots for Dr Pepper, Plymouth, Buick, Ford.

CHEVROLET Chevy pickup trucks can haul houses. Dramatic evidence of power, even if you don't have to move your house today.

Toyota, and Gleem, among others, and he has just written the script for a sit-com called *Future Stars*. Today he's playing the role of director of a Broadway show. He enters again, snapping out his lines, "OK, girls, we got to work on the step. We've got one hour to go. Bop bop bop." Four girls climb up on four pianos, and four piano players prepare to play.

When that take is finished, Paula Lynn, the lead dancer, pops her bubble gum. One of the piano players, wearing a sweater vest and red shirt, chews gum; another, who has on a wild check shirt with red, yellow, green, and orange stripes, just stares. A third one chats with Paula Lynn. The fourth twists his frizzy hair.

"OK," says Levenson. "Now, Tony, this time after you say, 'OK, girls,' pause a few seconds."

"OK, Fred."

Tony enters again. He is too fast. Levenson tells him to start again: "Don't go by the camera noise." Finally Tony gets the pause, the smile, the bop bop right.

Levenson says, "We're going to record the sound now." The execs who have been whispering shush each other. "Tony, hold it right back there. Can we kill the overheads for a while?" There is a rattle of metal louvers, the lights go out, the fans come on. "We had paper towels right there—what'd you do with them?"

The script girl answers, "Prop man came and took them." The assistant director finds the towels—they are needed to polish the front piano. The assistant director polishes it. The lights go back on. The dancers take their positions. "OK, let's hold all the talk, and lock it up."

The crowd quiets down. A prop man waves an incense burner around, just out of camera range, spreading some smoke to create an authentically foggy atmosphere. The audiotape recording man yells, "Speed!" The assistant director says, "Ready, actors." Tony comes in, gives his rap, the girls get up on the pianos and stretch.

"You're moving a little fast, Tony."

"OK."

"And can you move this equipment? You're in the mirror." Two men standing behind the director with a metal box edge out of their own reflection. "Oh, and Paula, you got up a little too soon. And you had a bubble last time. You didn't have a bubble. Make the bubble early. Now who was doing smoke? It looked like the place was on fire. Lay off the smoke. John, you're in my shot. OK, Paula, I want to stay with you. Somebody fix Paula's hair." Two women rush in and comb and primp Paula's hair. "OK, Paula, let me see your first position." Paula has an ex-

---

DANNON In this spot Mom congratulates her 89-year-old son on eating Dannon yogurt, then the whole village of centenarians celebrates with native dances. To find the oldsters, admen flew into a small village in Soviet Georgia.

pressionless face. She is just working. "Up quicker. You've got to get up quicker. Good. Now I want to do one more shot. It's not on the slate. We'll back-slate it. OK, honey, get your foot up—action. OK, stand up, please. OK, cut. OK, put your feet together. Let me see the taps."

Paula protests: "I'm trying not to put my heel down."

"Let me see you check that strap. That'll bring your heel up. OK. That'll do it." He films. "Cut. No, one more time. Get ready, love. Keep the feet together." He films again. "Good. Action. Good. Cut. OK, relax. OK, take a few minutes."

The script girl says, "End slate MO 2." She writes that down.

"Can we get some air in here?" calls Levenson. "Turn on the air conditioning. Kill this bank of lights. It's not in the next shot."

The executives start joking about the smoke effects. "Can we get some more of that incense? I like that."

"You like that smell?"

Now six men come forward and study the piano tops for any signs of scratches. If there are any, the whole commercial gets scrubbed. Their claim—that St. Regis's material can pro-

ANNOUNCER: His mother was very pleased.

tect the pianos—goes kaput, and the lawyers will keep the commercial off the air. No marks so far.

Someone asks Levenson, "How much of the commercial do you have on film so far?"

"About five seconds."

Now Paula tap dances for a minute on top of the piano, while the actors playing the supposed producer, his tarty, over-eye-glassed girl friend, and two quaking aides watch, miming worry that the dancer will ruin a $15,000 rented piano. The producer is being played by a Scottish actor, Douglas Gordon, and he reminds me of Robert Morley: fat, able to mug an aristocratic sneer, a pro. Meanwhile the real producer for the commercial is actually worrying that the polyethylene film protecting the pianos may get too hot in these lights and pop open.

When Paula has finished, the prop crew peels back the film very gingerly. "Lawyer!"

Herbert Kaplan, the lawyer hired by the ad agency, walks up. He inspects the piano top. He nods, "It works." No scratches.

"It's OK! The lawyer says it's OK!" The executives laugh and applaud. Someone says, "We got our legal proof, so now he won't get in the way any more."

Everyone relaxes because now the FTC, FCC, and the networks will accept the claim that if you dance on a piano top for forty-five seconds using this polyethylene film, you won't scar the surface. The commercial can go on the air. To celebrate, we break for lunch.

When I come back from lunch, one pianist is playing a sentimental song I don't recognize, and another is adding notes to his own score. The guy who polishes the mirror is yawning. An engineer slumped in a wooden folding chair says, "Over on 44th Street there's a place they sell yogurt. It's the greatest yogurt in the world. 44th and Third. It's spectacular yogurt."

The dumpy woman he is talking to is not impressed. "I read an article about it; it doesn't do anything for you. How's your family, John?"

"Fine."

"They getting married?"

"I only have one kid—daughter. She's getting married in December."

"Time goes by."

"My, yes."

"Mine are all married. And my husband died a year ago yesterday. So I'm back where I began. You wonder where it all went, what the point is."

Levenson comes in. "You got the bubble gum?"

"Naw," says a whey-faced aide.

"I bought bubble gum and those cigars—they're downstairs. Get 'em." The aide goes.

One dancer tightens her shoes. Paula Lynn puts her hands on her haunch and tugs at the pink top she has on over her purple tights. Levenson says, "You know what we're doing? We're doing frames thirteen through fifteen, the dancing."

A pianist asks, "What music? You told us you'd tell us." Levenson and he mutter together and find the music. The assistant director goes behind the black drapes, calling, "All the actors, all the actors." The actors bunch up behind the camera, pulling on their shoes, then take their places.

"OK, this is a wide shot," says Levenson. He turns to Tony. "You're just watching them dance, and we'll cut to your line." The audio man replays the sound from before, and the girls dance as the producer and his girl friend come in and stare. "Good. Do me a favor, Muriel, clean her shoes." The wardrobe lady polishes Paula's taps. "OK, roll me in, I'll tell you when to stop." Two grips push the heavy wagon forward, complete with camera and director. "Tony, your position, please."

"Where is that?"

"Over here. Yes. Now, I'm sorry, sir, what is your first name?"

"Doug," says the lordly "producer."

"OK, Doug, come closer to the piano. OK, big fella, move behind him. Yeah, move that stage light back toward the 750—yes, camera left a touch more, you got it. Can the other fella

come in more?" The two actors playing stage hands reading the papers move closer. "Take the girl friend's glasses off. On, off, it's OK with me."

A woman in brown suede says, "They're not the right glasses."

"Muriel! Get the rhinestone glasses. And can you get that E.U.E. bag out of there? OK, why don't we light up that green smoke? Love, I don't need dancing."

Tony asks, "Fred, do I have to have the sweater on? Is this later?"

"Yes, yes. OK, get the smoke started. Kill the air conditioning. How long are you going to play?" he asks the pianists.

"How long do you want it?" asks the lead pianist.

"All through. OK, Doug, don't let your girl friend block you. Lights, please." Now he turns to Paula. "What we are doing, my dear, is the body shot—forty-five seconds of tap dancing." He raises his voice. "Give me more smoke! Blast it in there! Give me some more smoke, it looks absolutely too clean. Come on, smoke, you're not even on my set. OK, props, I want you to rotate the light stands—no, too far—no, the other way. OK, hold it. How are we doing on the smoke out there?"

A voice from behind the mirror says: "One minute, please."

We wait five minutes. The director calls, "How long is that going to take?"

A chief executive in brown corduroy pants, red and white shirt, and blue blazer says, "Held up by smoke."

Another exec says, "Just send Stafford back there with a cigar."

A trenchcoat with a moustache arrives: "CBS is in last place," he remarks to no one in particular.

The smoke comes. The lights go on. They film Paula tap dancing for forty-five seconds.

In the next shot the actors playing aides to the producer peel back the polyethylene film. "Now when you peel it back, make sure it's underneath my lens. Don't block my lens. And as you see it's OK, Doug, you will light the cigar. You're serious, you see it's OK, you smile, then you give your line." They try it once. "OK, Doug, read the line quicker, don't drag it out. More pompous. Yes. Can you give it to me a little more Shakespearean? And Tony, big smile. After all, he's the backer. If he doesn't like it, nobody works. So everybody's relieved, right? OK, we're set. Give him another cigar."

The producer now has another line to say: "Incredible." They go over that three times. Levenson says, "That incredible reading was fine, but this time do it slightly faster."

"The word *incredible*?"

"Yes, and your hands should shake right after the handshake."

"OK, I see. I cut the smile and go directly to *incredible*."

"Right. And you guys in the back, I'd like you to react more, too."

Through each revision, Levenson has added suspense, bigger emotional reactions, more detailed background, more smiles, more eyeball-rolling. "Fellas in back—I want to see you straining to see, too. One more time!" Discriminating by half a second, adding one tiny gesture each time, Levenson puts together the scene as if he were assembling a machine. Stafford Ordahl watches, pulling on his Honduran cigar. Someone knocks a cup of Coke over, and it drips onto the footlights. A crew member says, "They've spilled more damn Cokes on my lights."

As I leave, I hear Levenson saying, "Break it with more feeling. It wasn't sharp enough. Just your eyes—now get angry—good, just your eyes—now more hurt."

This shoot took two days—fast, considering how complex the setup was. Swift Butterball Turkeys once took two days—and five dozen turkeys—just to get one shot in which the meat seems to slice like custard.

Sometimes a rush drives costs up. Bryan Olesky, a rising star, says, "I have spent fortunes on commercials. When I was at Wells, Rich, Greene, I did a thirty-second commercial that cost the client over $130,000. It was such a simple commercial—one man in the first-class lounge of a 747. It could have been shot very inexpensively, but the client—TWA—needed it very quickly. The expenses involved—oh, my God—casting on both coasts, flying people back and forth, the logistics of putting together a commercial in two weeks. One hundred and thirty thousand is a lot of money, but not when you think of the profits in the airline business, when somebody is paying three or four hundred dollars a ticket, and you have three or four hundred people on the plane, and you're talking about three or four flights a day. Maybe that's why the commercials are the best thing on TV."

And sometimes you have to rent a hangar to build your sets. Olesky says, "I remember a job that caused a producer to leave the business. We were shooting some TWA commercials in a big sound studio in California. It was a very big-budget job—we were shooting a whole packet of commercials. We had built, well, almost an entire city. We had mock-ups of the 747 on one side, mock-ups of the 707 on the other, mock-ups of an older plane on another—we had sets built in different parts of the studio. We were in there almost a week shooting, and the thing had been built during the week before we came. The producer had been there to supervise the building. We shot our four commercials, two sixties and two thirties. We wrapped. We did all this to produce three minutes. I remember this producer and I were sitting on this piece of wood in the middle of this huge vast studio, with the workers like ants all over the place, tearing down what he had just built for over two hundred thousand dollars. They were ripping it apart. He looked at me, and he said, 'I think this is gonna be my last job. I can't take the unreality of it. I'm living in a fantasy world. I come out here, I spend a fortune, two hundred and fifty thousand dollars—more than the average working man makes in twenty years—to build this, we shoot some film, and I tear it down, and I'm off to do something else for Alka-Seltzer! The unreality of it, the money of it, I can't face it.'"

Such men are rare in this business, where most writers and directors dream of going on location. One writer came up with the idea of putting a five-story box of detergent out on an open plain, to be worshipped by hundreds of people. They went to Yugoslavia to build the thing, and as soon as it was built, rain came. For three weeks. The box fell over. So they went to Israel. They built another box. Protesters showed up: the film crew was desecrating an ancient shrine. More delays, more costs, no spot. Another writer decided to show a Chevy floating down the Grand Canal in Venice. They put the car on a raft that sank under the surface of the water

DOLPHIN PRODUCTIONS Switching, punching, patching, and transferring images, Bob Blansky and Bruce Davis create abstract electronic designs for another spot.

but still floated; by putting the towboat far enough in front, the director made it look as if the Chevrolet really was driving down the canal. They show Italians saying things which the subtitles translate as, "Look at the beautiful car." That commercial made a brief splash.

When Daniel & Charles agency sent people from the Lee Lacy studio to England to shoot a commercial demonstrating the "crushed look" of Wohl Shoes, they borrowed the Duke of Bedford's front lawn, sprayed it with green paint, added two thousand daisies, built a bunker for the cameraman, rented a Sherman tank, and had the tank run over the shoes several times. Said the Duke afterwards, "If it was a crushed look they were after, they should have seen my face when I saw my lawn."

One scriptwriter found out that in Soviet Georgia, where some people live to be 167 years old, they eat a lot of yogurt. In a few weeks an ad team looked up a town, booked flights, moved in, interviewed some friendly old folks who could claim a century or so working outdoors as beekeepers, shepherds, or gardeners. Most did eat yogurt—and vegetables—but not much meat. They drank dry wine. The film crew gave out Dannon's yogurt and filmed the centenarians eating it and dancing in their native outfits. They made several commercials from these cute scenes. One ends: "89-year-old Renan Topagua liked Dannon so much he ate two cups. That pleased his mother very much." She smiles and pats him. Soviet scientists were annoyed at the popularity of this commercial and—flat-footedly taking it seriously—argued that yogurt was not the only thing that keeps people alive for a century. Hard work outdoors and the respect of an extended family are at least as important as yogurt, stated a doctor from the Kiev Institute of Gerontology: "The person made things, and he was happy."

Some commercials don't need to be shot on location to get astonishing effects, though.

Some, shot from airplanes, often involve hours of ticklish preparation and testing, but they let us see things as if we were birds—or golf balls. Leger Katz Partners decided that we might want to see what a golf course looks like from on top of the ball as it spins down the first hole. And so we do. *Whack!* We go up fast, just behind a Maxfli ball spinning backwards as we look down at the Braemar Golf Club in Tarzana, California. The Maxfli is really a basketball painted white and mounted on a rotisserie slung under a helicopter. The camera is in the helicopter. Even more extravagant, Mohasco once made up a giant Mohawk carpet, unrolled it the length of the local airport, and had a plane land on it.

Such spots encourage us to imagine life the way kids do: planes can land on the rug, we can fly, and cars can, too—until we drop them. Jack Keil, at Dancer-Fitzgerald Sample agency, wanted the new Toyota to float in space, but he didn't want any trick photographer, and he needed the finished commercial in a month. He hired "one of the best riggers in the business," who took a big truck and built a stanchion on it with a strong steel arm that went out like a question mark. "Now this arm did a dogleg to hold the car. And inside the car we put gears. When we activated this electronically, it would turn. We

could shoot underneath, back to front; it could tilt and turn and twist, and we could go underneath it.

"But when we first rigged this out in the field, and he yelled, 'OK, let her go,' as soon as he said that, whoop, the truck went up in the air, and the car dropped. 'Oh, well,' he said. So then he put eight tons on the front of his truck to hold it down. Then we worried about the bar holding the car. We went into the studio and cut through the floor and put chains around the axles of the truck and chained it to bedrock. So then the car starts doing that turning and bucking some twenty feet up in the air, and we start filming. We had dummies up in the car— we couldn't get real people up there with all the gears, and besides, no person would get in that thing—and every once in a while the car would tilt and a dummy's arm would fly out." The commercial's "look" was finished off by adding Christmas tree lights on black drapes to look like stars.

Extravagant fantasies like this are simply bigger, realer, more expensive versions of a child's knocking a toy off a table or skimming it over the water in the bath. In a minor extravaganza of its own, Volkswagen once drove a car off a pier and onto the water: *onto* the water, because

it floated. Floated? It skipped! In fact, it shot so far out to sea they had to use a motorboat to bring it back. Ford figured their car was just as airtight and rented a pool. They lowered the car into the water. It sank. More expensive are the operations in which the producer plays doctor on a car, taking it apart. Of course, when a child takes something apart, it stops. But why can't it go on moving, in pieces? Several productions have spent hours of mechanics' time recreating this fantasy. Chevrolet once cut an Impala in half lengthwise and drove it down the street. Extra wheels and tiny gas tanks were added on the inside, and the ad agency hired a midget as driver. Such effects may look like trick photography, but they aren't. They appeal to our unconscious, which is always a child, because they make "real" what we previously only imagined. Sometimes this "reality" is impossible to achieve; then the Alice-in-Wonderland effect must be put across with the camera man's magic: When the tiny woman walks among West Bend pressure cookers twice as tall as she is or leans against the buttons of Sanyo radios as big as a

PEPTO-BISMOL This spot depends on video trickery from Dolphin Computer Animation: a twist of the knob, and your stomach balloons.

house, one camera shoots the product, another shoots the spokeswoman, very far off; and, by pressing a button labeled "key," the producer "keys" the woman into the pot. But whether they do it in reality or in the video gear, most producers insist on making the unreal as real as possible—for themselves and their lawyers, not just for us.

Some inner experiences, though, cannot be shown photographically—the feeling of an attack of indigestion, for instance. So the producer may turn to a computer animation studio like Dolphin Studios in New York for help. With Pepto-Bismol, for example, we see a sorry-looking executive worrying his eyebrows, his pencil, his manila folder, his mouth. Behind him a guy is washing the windows. The executive looks up with white-eyed horror. He turns green, literally, and says, "Indi-i-i" as his ghostly form bubbles like a fun-house mirror—"gestion." The window washer stares at him. And the announcer says, "Pepto-Bismol" as the label runs across the screen and erases the scene. Now a woman is sitting on a white sofa with her terrier. "Indi-"—she turns purple and her swollen belly wiggles toward the dog—"gestion." The dog gets up; he backs off, fearful. Now a construction worker gets hit: his belly fills out in orange. Then the logo's words get coated with purple liquid: it pours down inside the white letters that spell out: COATS, SOOTHES, RELIEVES. How's it done? First the Dolphin crew records the image of a real environment for the background. Then they place the actor who is about to suffer in front of a blue curtain. His image is fed into an analogue computer which allows Dolphin to manipulate his shape to express a particular form of digestive distress—rubbery bones, billowing belly. Appropriate colors, such as purple, green, and orange, are washed over the actor at the same time. Then, showing the background throughout, the Dolphin team assembles the pieces so that we can

PEPSI-COLA A tumbler does a flip while a bicycler zips by; thanks to flashy production techniques, we see the afterglow as well.

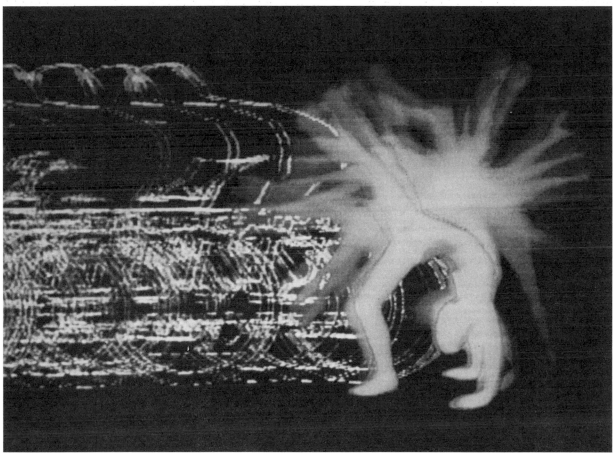

watch the real picture dissolve into the "unreal" one while the surroundings remain unchanged. The entire scene is then wiped away by a huge bottle of Pepto-Bismol while the announcer reverently repeats the product's name.

Even more spectacular electronic effects mimic the rush of information, stored images, and linked ideas brought up to consciousness by psychedelic drugs. For Pepsi a bicycler rides across the screen, in outline. He leaves behind about twenty afterimages, white lines that trail him, moving behind him. In this wake of electrons, a blue tumbler—partly real, partly abstract—flips into place from the right. From the left, about fifty orange basketball players rush in and become one; from the right, twenty hockey play-

ers lift strangely glowing blue sticks; now the basketball players shoot. All dissolve as a bottle top tips toward us, with the Pepsi label. We open that and see real pictures through it: a golfer, tennis doubles, scuba divers, then the fast-cut disco scenes reduce into the bottle again. We hear a loud sound of pouring. As we hear the gurgle, a line forming waves rises through the picture; what shows below is a picture of Pepsi bottles on ice, revolving. The circular motion gets mimicked by a blue mist that ebbs in from all sides, narrowing down so we can only see the bottles through an oval in the middle of a solid blue field. Then, from the lower right, blurred letters rush up, tossing off loose electrons, to form the logo: Pepsi.

The producer of such commercials presides over a fairy world in which he uses dozens of people, tons of time and talent, and hundreds of feet of film to create the illusion that, with a certain product, we can fly like a golf ball or drive on water. If asked why he does this, a production chief might answer, "To make money and to sell the product."

But for most of these grown-ups working all these hours, eating so many bad doughnuts, the real product is the commercial. Yes, it may move paper towels—later. But for the production crew, such results seem transcendental. And what kind of product have they made? Forty-five feet of film, or nine hundred frames of videotape, when edited. An artificial universe, in which we can indulge in dreams of having magical powers to change our size, shape, location, car, even our visual perceptions by swallowing something, saying a rhyme, or buying a shiny object.

When we watch these spots, we're not spending time on comparative shopping or intellectual testing of rival claims. So what are we doing? Radical critics of television point out that television executives tend to view television as a device to collect thousands of viewers, a "product" to be sold to the advertisers. But in fact, the commercials are also part of the entertainment—the best part if we define *entertainment* as the fantasy satisfaction of more or less unconscious impulses.

From this point of view, the writers, actors, director, and producer of a commercial may all be seen as unwitting partners with the audience in a vast dance of culture as we perform and applaud our own inner life writ large and bright in thirty-second fragments. As emblems for our collective unconscious and as the ironic end-result of our constant financial interaction, commercials may be America's most significant product.

One sign of how much we want to believe in commercials is the outrage we sometimes feel when we notice the illusion fraying at the edge. In general, we want them to be real, and if they aren't, we sue.

For example: Is this lying? Under the super-bright lights in a TV studio, real coffee often looks thin, so some producers slip molasses in the cup for the rich, dark look they want. In the heat of the studio, beer loses its head, and the glass loses its beads of moisture, so assistant directors have at times whipped up detergent on top and misted the outside every few minutes with a garden spray. In the glare of the lights, all soapy lather begins to wilt before the model's face is dry, so one director hired a home economist to whip up some egg whites to look like foaming shampoo. When the director ladled out the Campbell's soup, the meat and vegetables sank; rather than let viewers think the soup was thin, he put marbles under the chunky stuff. When Rapid Shave decided to shave sandpaper, the actor found the blade clogged: what to do? Glue sand on glass so that it looks like sandpaper, and lather it up; the sand came off without a glitch. Downy Fabric Softener wanted to show that towels are soft and springy after you wash with their product, so they dropped the bottle on a towel, and it bounced quite well, thanks to the sponge rubber hidden underneath. When Easy-Off boasted that it could clean windows better than its competitor, the director found the comparison worked better when he wiped the Easy-Off window but failed to wipe the competitor's. Hmmm.

Such cheap magic tends to send sales up for a few months, then backfires when people find that they can't shave their own sandpaper or bounce bottles off their towels. Mary Hartman may have been an archetypical consumer—her schedule: 8:15, Viva test; 8:30, cut Dove soap in half. Disappointed consumers and angry competitors write their congressmen, who in turn call up the Federal Trade Commission, which sometimes cries foul. But policing the exaggerations, suggestions, half-truths, vague claims, weasel words, and occasional outright lies in over 30,000 network commercials a year, plus another 30,000 or so on local stations, boggles even the federal bureaucracy. So they threaten, and they make up rules, and occasionally—rarely—they take some recalcitrant company to court over persistent misrepresentations.

To avoid any more federal supervision than this, the ad world has come up with its own version of self-regulation. Any complaints from injured rivals or consumers now go to the National Advertising Division of the Council of Better Business Bureaus; the NAD demands that the advertiser submit proof of any claims, and if the NAD does not find the proof sufficient, they ask the advertiser to withdraw the ads or change them. If the advertiser refuses, the case gets bumped up to the National Advertising Review Board. There a five-man panel, made up of three typical advertisers, one agency guy, and one public member, hears the debate and makes a decision, either okaying the ads or urging the advertiser to withdraw or change the ads. If the advertiser still refuses, the whole file gets sent to the FTC for possible investigation, warning, or prosecution. It can all take years, and usually any offending spot has outlived its usefulness before the procedure is completed, so the sponsor can gracefully offer to withdraw it, without suffering any cash loss. This grand round robin of complaint and discussion tends to act like a cushion, then, not a sheriff.

But its decisions do seep down into the consciousness of copywriters as "sort-of" rules, as danger signals, as warnings of what not to write about or claim. As a result, in trying to make a unique selling promise, they must wiggle and waggle and duck and dodge a lot to think up an attractive line that will not upset the NAD, NARB, FTC—or the networks, who have their own censors looking over every commercial before it goes on the air.

What happens down at the bottom of this chain, at the NAD? Surprisingly, many claims get substantiated by independent testing labs. Play-Doh claimed that a child could press out a rope of Play-Doh, a modeling compound, and squeeze it into the shape of an ice-cream cone. Could kids really do this? Sure enough, tests showed that children from three to five could do it. Let the spots continue. But what about Freedent, a chewing gum that boasted that "It won't stick to most dental work"? Independent researchers gave the gum to people wearing dentures and watched them chew; the respondents chewed each of four types of gum, once in the morning, and once in the afternoon. The other gums got stickier as time went on, but everyone agreed Freedent didn't stick. Even dentists couldn't find any residue. So Freedent was free to go on chewing our ears off on TV. Then there's that Krazy Glue commercial: Can the glue really hold a man's helmet—not to mention the man wearing the helmet—to a steel bar dangling in the air? David Horowitz, on his half-hour NBC-TV show called *Consumer Buyline,* tried to glue a hard hat (just the hat) to a beam, using Krazy Glue; it didn't work, so they tried it again, and it still didn't work. Krazy Glue stopped advertising on station KNBC for a few months after that. But the NAD found that tests using lots of different materials, temperatures, humidity, and setting time proved the tensile strength per square inch of Krazy Glue was "far in excess of that required for the TV demonstration."

A few sponsors do change their ads under NAD pressure. Western Airlines flies to the sunbelt, and they advertised throughout the North that "It's summer in Los Angeles" or "in San Diego" or in other places in southern California. The NAD says, "A question was raised concerning the appropriateness of the word 'summer' in this advertising. While it was recognized that the Southwest may generally have good weather in the winter months, this may not always be the case. Further, it was suggested that the word 'summer' specifies a particular time of year and at the time the advertising appeared, it was not really summer, but winter." But since the areas mentioned did have warm weather, the NAD suggested the airlines bill them as "summer-like." With that silly change, the spots went back on the air. Rohm and Hass Company called its Vacor rat killer "America's Number One Rat Killer" until the NAD noted that a rival brand called d-Con had bigger sales; the NAD redefined the term *Number One,* so that for copywriters, *Number One* now means best seller, not best performer. Vacor abandoned the phrase.

Most advertisers drop ads if the NAD finds them "unsubstantiated." Rhodes Electric Piano claimed that their equipment was played by 82 percent of the musicians with hit records for 260 weeks in a row. When the NAD asked for proof, the company replied that, "For marketing reasons, these claims have been discontinued." And Cracker Jack put an old man on the air saying, "Kids haven't changed. But what's in some of the things they're nibbling, that's changed. Stabilizers and preservatives, like BHA, BHT. This is Cracker Jack . . . all natural ingredients . . . 100 percent natural. Nothing artificial. So don't worry, Mom—it's Cracker Jack." The NAD worried that this ad might imply to consumers that all stabilizers and preservatives are, by their nature, undesirable. Cracker Jack disagreed, but agreed to discontinue the commercial. (In this way, the NAD helped out the competition and prevented an embarrassingly public fight in court.)

HOWDY DOODY Until FTC rulings banned the practice, hosts of children's shows could plug products; shown here, Buffalo Bob with his puppet, Howdy Doody, in 1952.

Do people believe there are mermaids who recommend tuna fish? Yes, whined a complainant from outside the NAD. (The NAD hides the names of complainants in their files.) The jingle for Chicken of the Sea tuna sang, "Ask any mermaid you happen to see, 'What's the best tuna?' Chicken of the Sea." The complainant tested viewers' comprehension of this spiel and argued that people thought the "best tuna" claim was a statement of fact. But NAD laughed at the test design, and called the mermaids' advice "puffery" and therefore (thank goodness) "not subject to the test of truth and accuracy." Puffery is defined by the NAD as harmless exaggeration that audiences recognize as such; any clearer definition is, evidently, impossible. So the idea of puffery opens a loophole large enough for a mermaid to swim through.

Overall, the NAD, which was set up during 1971, had handled 1241 challenges by June 30, 1977. Not all of these dealt with TV commercials; some involved print ads, radio ads, or outdoor billboards. In 459 cases the claims were found to be substantiated; in 412 more cases the ads were changed or dropped; 66 cases were still dragging on. And 291 cases were closed for "administrative reasons," whatever they are. Only 13 challenges got sent along to the NARB. So most of the time the NAD acted as a buffer for the first complaints, backing up the advertiser or debating the matter until the spot got changed or dropped, often having outlived its usefulness.

What happens when the NAD's diplomacy cannot resolve a battle between the sponsor and some complainant? The case goes to the National Advertising Review Board. The initials NARB have a magisterial ring, rather like those of the National Labor Relations Board; but the NARB does not have the force of law. It can make suggestions, though, and for most copywriters, those hints tend to become rules. According to William Ewen, who was executive director of the NARB until he retired in 1975, the NARB began because, "During the late sixties and early seventies the gathering forces of consumerism began mounting well-publicized attacks on the business community for alleged lack of responsibility in almost every activity that affected the consumer directly or indirectly." And soon, "The advertising business feared the hasty passage of laws that would severely limit its ability to perform effectively as a vital part of the marketing process." So the ad community created the NARB. Not so much for the consumer, then, but to keep the consumer from getting a chance to set rules for advertising, to preserve the general reputation of all business, and to prevent nasty infighting between competitors from bursting into real court cases, the NARB was set up before Congress thought of it. The NARB became the Miss Etiquette of commercials.

In one early case a complainant bitched that the commercial for Hershey's Krackel candy bars exaggerated the sounds a child would "hear" chewing a Krackel. Was Hershey falsely promising "aural thrills"? The NARB said yes, the sounds are exaggerated, but the candy does make a crackling sound. Spot okayed. Someone else complained about Zenith Radio's TV spot that claims, "Every color TV Zenith makes is built right here in the U.S. by Americans like these." It turned out that 14.5 percent of the components came from abroad, and the NAD had found this advertising "misleading." When the NAD appealed to the NARB, Zenith gave in and withdrew the ads.

Sometimes a whole product area gets into a dogfight. Kal Kan got angry because a competitor kept sneering at them for adding cereal and other natural foods to their dogfood; eager to point out that dogs need a balanced diet, not just meat, Kal Kan counterattacked, stressing that their ingredients were natural and healthy as opposed to the synthetic ingredients of their competitors. Consumers got the idea that the

synthetic chemicals and supplements might be harmful, so the NARB got Kal Kan to drop the spots. But soon someone complained that Ralston Purina's Chuck Wagon Dinner for Dogs showed what were called "tender juicy chunks." These looked like meat but turned out to be soybean mash. New copy was written after the NAD bucked it up to the NARB. Still, Alpo stressed the meat in its product so much that people thought it was all meat, even though a copywriter had carefully included the ambiguous phrase, "meat by-products, beef and balanced nutrition." The NARB held that this phrase did not show that the product included flour from soybeans. Alpo rewrote the spot.

Capitalists often boast that our economic system depends on competition, but until recently advertisers tacitly agreed that it was better not to name the competition too baldly. Back in 1922, the Better Business Bureau said, "Advertising should be positive and constructive." How come? "Disparagement invites retaliation. Few, if any, advertised products are perfect. The advertiser who is attacked can invariably find something to criticize in the product of his competitor. As 'knocking copy' becomes general in an industry, the sum total of its effect is to unsell the entire industry to the public." So we were treated to tests that showed M&M's candy melting in your mouth while Brand X melted in your hand and there were ridiculous comparisons of one brand of margarine to a mysterious "high-priced spread." But in 1972 staffers at the Federal Trade Commission decided that if the networks would just allow comparative ads, consumers would begin to hear real comparisons. Robert Pitofsky, director of the FTC's Bureau of Consumer Protection, said that Brand X comparisons, in which the competitor was not named, "prevent the consumer from receiving information which is relevant and useful in making an informed choice between competing products and may in some cases result in the consumer being misled or deceived." His staff talked CBS and ABC into allowing such ads; NBC had never banned them. Within a year comparative ads in prime time went from 0 to 8 percent. By 1976, 25 percent of the ads reviewed by the NAD and the NARB identified competitors; in most of these cases, the complainants were the competitors who had been named.

Alberto-Culver took Gillette to court for claiming that Gillette's cream rinse Tame was superior to Alberto Balsam; they sued for $7 million. Coke knocked Pepsi; Behold boasted it could beat Pledge; the NARB found, after 300 pages of testimony, that Schick's Flexamatic electric razor was not necessarily good enough to "beat Norelco, Remington and Sunbeam for closeness." Andrew Kershaw, chairman of Ogilvy & Mather, calls such ads "stupidly provocative ... the kind of mud-slinging that has hitherto been the special preserve of politics." Meanwhile, Duracell batteries keep the pink bunny going longer than any other battery. And the Big Blue pad (S.O.S Soap Pad) beats Pink Pad in a big convention by 2 to 1 in the voting. Peugeot wins over a skier in the downhill slalom. Conair shows a split screen. On the left a woman is giggling, having fun with a Water Pic shower massage; on the right a woman shows up with the Conair Waterfingers: as she massages her scalp, brushes her body, and giggles indecently, the woman in the next-door shower stall sinks into a depression because she does not have as much to play with.

"Greasy dirt!" The announcer runs his finger over the white enamel panel above the stove. "It's a no-no in the kitchen." We come up close and he points at us. "How do you solve that problem?" We cut to a woman who says, "I

WATERFINGERS BY CONAIR Split-screen comparisons became popular after the FTC started pushing the networks to allow one-to-one competition in spots. Here Waterfingers outmassage Water Pik.

ANNOUNCER: With Water Pik's Shower Massage, you can have a lot of fun in the shower.

And a body brush to massage your body.

With Conair's Waterfingers, you can have just as much fun in the shower.

But with Waterfingers, you get a scalp brush to stimulate your scalp.

And to make it even more fun, it costs less.

Waterfingers by Conair. The shower that gives you more than a good time.

would say ammonia." Another, "I would say ammonia, straight." We cut to a shot of both ladies, standing there ill at ease, fingers locked at the waist, with logos superimposed over them: Mrs. McLaughlin, Mrs. Butler. Off camera he asks, "What would you say if I told you ammonia's good for some jobs, but not for greasy dirt? Top Job cleans greasy dirt ammonia can't." We see their reaction: "Terrific!" "I don't believe it." He says, "Let's see what happens." They turn and we zip into the test. They each rub a different panel, one labeled ammonia, the other Top Job. Mrs. Butler, the doubter, says, "That's amazing. And the Top Job was diluted. The Top Job side, there's no dirt, there's no streaky marks left, and on the ammonia side there are still streak marks left because there is still grease left." Mrs. Butler looks off camera for approval. Now the two ladies stand together; Top Job as big as they are floats between them, and the announcer reads the words below their knees: "For Tough Greasy Dirt!"

The network censors were not happy with comparative ads. In 1975 CBS rejected 238 out of 490 comparative commercials submitted to them. "CBS feels that comparative advertising is not always making for a better informed consumer," said Jack Hinton, who okays commercials. "We don't like it, most advertisers don't like it, and our mail indicates consumers don't like it."

And as the NARB worked out the rules for comparative ads, they found numerous spots improper. A toilet bowl cleaner claimed that it "disinfects and deodorizes better," but tests only showed that it deodorized more—whatever that means; this was a case of "misleading language." Other ads tested the product in situations not encountered in a suburban house; compared their own new data with the competitor's out-of-date data; claimed that they were ahead of the competitor, when it turned out they were only ahead alphabetically in the Yellow Pages.

After tut tuts, these ads stopped.

But the NARB allowed one mouthwash to claim it kept breath fresh twice as long, because tests indeed showed it lasted 105 minutes compared to the competitor's 45 minutes. One snack-pack pudding turned out to be chosen by consumers as "creamier, more chocolatey, and better tasting" in real tests. And Bounty paper towels really can hold up a coffee cup, they found. So these spots survive.

In its leaflets, the NARB says a sponsor should ask questions, though, before going on the air with a comparative spot: Can you prove superiority in all circumstances? Have you refrained from claiming overall superiority just because you test better on one element? Are you comparing the same grade of product, not your best, against their cheapest? Can the consumer figure out what you mean by *extra*? If you compare the two products at work, are the lighting conditions identical, and are the label instructions really followed? If your diet soft drink has two calories, and your competitor's has four, do you avoid potentially misleading—though true—claims like "50 percent fewer calories"? Do the test results really support all your claims? Can most people get the same results at home? Have you bought enough time to tell the whole story? And, finally, "In doing comparative advertising, are we truly helping the consumer make a better-informed choice by presenting comparison facts that are significant, understandable, and useful? Or are we simply knocking the competitor product without making a genuine claim to superiority in respects which are important to the consumer?"

Anyone who thinks the latter must now reckon with a 1976 U.S. Supreme Court decision which struck down a Virginia law prohibiting the advertising of prices by pharmacies. The Court's opinion said that "Advertising, however tasteless and excessive it sometimes may seem, is nonetheless dissemination of information as to who is producing and selling what product, for what reason, and at what price. So long as we preserve a predominantly free enterprise economy, the allocation of our resources in large measure will be made through numerous private economic decisions. It is a matter of public interest that those decisions, in the aggregate, be intelligent and well-informed. To this end, the free flow of commercial information is indispensable." Although the Justices maintained that "some forms of commercial speech regulation are surely permissible," they in effect extended the First Amendment, guaranteeing free speech, to cover advertisers, although for sixty years the FTC had assumed that ads were *not* protected by the Constitution. And now, with the Supreme Court's opinion in mind, lower courts are questioning whether regulations of bodies like the Federal Trade Commission may not have a "chilling effect" upon the exercise of vital First Amendment rights. To protect against this, courts are saying that such regulations cannot be vague but must be narrowly specific, and the burden of justifying any regulation or restriction rests with the government.

The climate has turned against regulation. President Carter's drive for a consumer agency died without much quivering. His bill to allow consumers to file class-action suits against companies they suspect of violating FTC rules got squashed. The Chamber of Commerce feels pleased at having stalled these and other consumer protection bills, and some execs are even suggesting that regulations should be justified all over again, from the base zero.

Still, by lecture and press release, the FTC has managed to nudge advertisers into these comparative ads, and Tracy Westen, deputy direc-

TRACY WESTEN Activist Deputy Director of the Bureau of Consumer Protection, he has pushed the staff to come up with a strong medicine for advertisers of sweets.

tor of the FTC's Bureau of Consumer Protection, argues that these ads provide more information than "unilateral or traditional ads." Westen agrees that such ads may provoke angry fisticuffs in the marketplace, but, "This is fine." Such competition, like warfare, reveals "maximum truth." The Pepsi–Coke war, he thinks, taught consumers to be cautious about accepting test results, an opinion not shared by the head of the Council of Better Business Bureaus, who complained that comparative ads have "further damaged the credibility of advertising with equal negative effect on the mores of civilized business behavior," and called them an example of "jungle morality, paying lip service to competition, but placing an impossible burden on both consumers and business."

The advertisers' irritability at FTC actions may stem from the fact that the federal agency is often tougher on the industry than the industry's own watchdogs are. In court cases brought by the FTC several companies have suffered heavy fines. The FTC told Geritol to stop claiming that its product was an effective treatment for tiredness, loss of strength, run-down feelings, nervousness, or irritability. Geritol didn't stop, so Judge Constance Baker Motley ordered the J. B. Williams Company to pay $301,000 in civil penalties, plus interest. The FTC told Firestone not to claim that its tires were safe under all conditions unless it could back up that claim with scientific proof. Firestone ran the ads, but not the tests, and got taken to court. The court set this penalty: Firestone had to spend $100,000 to make and pretest commercials warning that no tire is safe under all conditions, and $550,000 to show this spot on TV during prime time; plus another $100,000 for similar ads in *Time, Reader's Digest,* and *U.S. News & World Report.* And the FTC ordered Listerine to make a new set of ads admitting that "Listerine will not help prevent colds or sore throats or lessen their severity." Listerine countered that the FTC or-

der—which forced Listerine to say something it did not believe—was actually a violation of free speech. Called to intervene, the U.S. Circuit Court of Appeals waffled: "It merely requires certain statements which if not present in current and future advertisements would render these advertisements themselves part of a continuing deception of the public." Warner Lambert, the maker of Listerine, can appeal to the Supreme Court, but so far the FTC seems to have the support of all the courts in forcing advertisers to admit they lied in previous ads.

By going to administrative law courts, the FTC gave its denture rules the grip of real law. Polident had shown denture-wearers chewing fried chicken and eating corn on the cob, but the judge found that the spots implied Polident let denture-wearers eat *anything* without having their teeth fall out. The Block Drug Company agreed to change its jingle.

But the FTC can only attack what it sees as outright deceptions, so it is pleased to have the advertisers' own watchdog, the NARB, at work. Such self-regulation also keeps advertisers from being too blatant in their deceptions, particularly the verbal ones. Clearcut cases of tricky advertising are often taken care of by the NARB, so the FTC can try to focus its energy on cases that involve whole industries, or a common deceptive practice. As a result, the number of cases the FTC is hearing has dropped from 56 to 22 in two years.

The new chairman of the FTC, Michael Pertschuk, once wrote consumer protection laws when he was chief counsel of the Senate Commerce Committee. He has pushed for labels on appliances showing how much energy they use per hour, and for much stricter guidelines about what can be said about over-the-counter drugs. But his main interest seems to be in formulating some program against commercials for sugary and fried cereals and candy, shown during children's shows. In fact, many liberals and con-

sumer advocates have taken up the cause of
children as the best way to regulate advertising
by law. So, while the complaints of adults tend
to be swallowed up and muffled in the paneled
rooms of the NAD and the NARB, the laments
of parents over kids crying, "Gimmeee!" will
probably resound in FTC hearings, justifying a
number of sharp regulations driving such ads
out of children's shows, and perhaps off the air.

Has the consumer been blessed by all this
activity? Not much. Have the ad agencies, the
sponsors, and the government together found a
way to keep imaginative copywriters from claiming more than they can prove? Not likely. The
human imagination is sharper, quicker, and
more tricky than the law, and just as a regulation closes off one path, the imagination dreams
up a balloon and floats past. Now the ad agency
must have a lawyer on the set to swear they
filmed the demonstration the way they claim;
but the demo itself may be just as silly or emotional, sexy or violent as ever; and no matter
how sober the words, the pictures may still make
the unconscious drunk.

As copywriters have already found, you can
tell the truth while suggesting much more. You
can still claim your beer is for people who want
something special, and no one can dispute you.
You can still call your product "the different
one." (Sure it's different; you spell your name
differently, and you have a green label). You
can always make another preemptive claim: most
coffee is grown in the mountains of Brazil, but
you can boast that yours is mountain grown, and
people will get the impression that only yours is
grown out there in the husky country. Or you
can avoid making any statements at all: just ask
questions ("Wouldn't you like to have a natural
hair spray?") or urge people to imagine what

MICHAEL PERTSCHUK   Head of the agency that
struggles like a behemoth to regulate or control the
sixty-odd thousand commercials aired each year.

they'll feel like using Rise. If you insist on making claims of superiority, just don't say superior to what: "We give you more." (More what?) Easy-Off Oven Cleaner gives you "33 percent more active ingredients than another popular spray oven cleaner." (Which one? What ingredient? What difference does it make?) "You can be sure, if it's Westinghouse." (Sure of what?) Pampers are for drier babies. Drier than what? So a few old tricks have been shucked—we can't put on a white coat and pretend to be a doctor any more, and cough medicines now have to be called "anti-tussives," but the ads still operate on the principle that it is enough to have a claim, any claim. Wiggly phrases are still snaking past us on the screen, beckoning the innocent to try a bite of this new, improved crunchy apple that gives you 85 percent more food energy (for which read calories) than the leading pain reliever (code for aspirin).

Light censorship cleans up the most obvious falsehoods so we can lose ourselves even more thoroughly in the thirty-second dream. Most people say they want the truth in advertising, and a few do, but most of the ads we look at are for products we will not use, or buy, so we tend to view commercials simply as entertainment. And in entertainment, we opt for science fiction over science, romance over information; even though we know we should hear a complete list of ingredients, we long for the magic show, when one pill changes a stomach from blue to white in five seconds. By laziness or design, then, we have arranged things so that the FTC, NAD, NARB, and networks can only vet the scripts for claims that can be proved or disproved. The wider realm of advertising—the vague promise, the implied benefit, the suggested delight— these candylands dazzle us despite regulation. How powerless censorship is against the forces of our collective unconscious!

"here's an adventure in every bowl of Alpha-bits," says an announcer.

A kid screams, "Dracula tried to get me."

The other kid says, "Oh no! What did you do?"

First kid: "I ate him." We see the letters that spell *Dracula* floating in a bowl of soup. As the kid slurps his spelling lesson, the monster behind him disintegrates.

Since most commercials seem to aim at the child in each of us, commercials for real children represent a special, and touchy, example of the conflicting pressures behind them all. Many middle-class parents, concerned that spots for unnatural cereals or fall-apart toys may hook their child on the lower class of food or toy, have banded together to change the rules for the one commercial in ten that is intended mainly for children. And, although the battle continues to seesaw back and forth between enemies and advocates of such spots, the activists have had sufficient success so that the commercials during the children's hours now seem distinctly duller than their cousins on prime time. Less exaggerated visually, less deceitful verbally, children's commercials are often more accurate representations of reality than such programs as *Isis, The Flintstones, Land of the Lost, Gilligan's Island,* or *Batman.* In addition, some commercials may actually teach children some useful skills for the post-modern era: how to read brand names, how to understand a TV story, how to discount repeated dubious claims and distorted pictures, how to comparison-test toys, and, at least at the moment, how to get excited over junk food.

Of the sixteen major non-Communist nations, only five allow any ads during children's programs, and until 1976, when we finally changed the rules, only the United States granted advertisers more time on children's programs than on adult shows. Only about 15 percent of children's television viewing is devoted to the kiddy shows on Saturday and Sunday morning; most of the time the children watch late afternoon and prime time shows, staying up until 9:00 P.M. Even at 11:00 P.M. broadcasters find there are at least a million children still tuned in. From age two to five, an average American child today will watch 30 hours of television a week; age six to eleven, 27 hours a week. So children under twelve experience almost five hours of spots a week, or over 30,000 commercials, most made for grown-ups, a year. By the end of high school, kids have spent more time "learning" from the tube than they have in a classroom.

Gerald Lesser, the professor from the Harvard Graduate School of Education who helped set up the fabulously profitable educational show *Sesame Street,* says, "We have never lacked reports, verified reports, of children who learn to read from commercials, quiz shows, or weather reports, or children who suddenly display some other advanced intellectual skill that they could only have learned from TV. Any adult can supply anecdotes about children whose first spoken words were 'Budweiser, Namath, Clairol, or Axion,' or who learned to spell Mickey Mouse or Batman before they could spell their own names." Lesser dismisses this knowledge as not worth knowing—"mindless advertising slogans." But he is so disgusted by the content that he overlooks the process of learning here.

Some children do learn to read and spell from commercials, because—unlike the shows they "interrupt"—commercials make an effort to show the viewer the name of a product while they say it out loud, and the commercial is rerun every day, so a child can put the message together gradually. Dr. Kenneth S. Goodman, professor of education at the University of Arizona, says, "Take a four-year-old to the supermarket. The youngster can identify 25 or 30 kinds of breakfast cereal. How did he or she learn this? By watching TV commercials, of course. Commercials are very effective at teaching preschoolers to

ANNOUNCER: John, John, Williamson, Williamson, Appelby, George Malone has a Waring Ice Cream Parlor right in his very home.

BOY: And that is very nice.

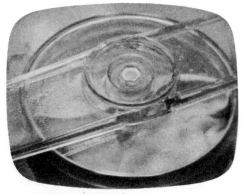

no special anything to it.

WARING Plugging its simplicity to children and adults, Waring adopts a child's point of view with its slogan: Waring's ice-cream maker is so easy, even a grown-up can do it.

It only needs regular table salt.

It only needs regular ice. It doesn't need to go in the fridge . . .

ANNOUNCER: No special salt.

No special ice . . .

The Waring Ice Cream Parlor makes ice cream so easy . . .

BOY: Even a grown-up can do it.

read, and so are other kinds of programming where there are quick flashes of written language. By the time they get to kindergarten, many kids have already made this connection between meaning and written symbols. That's the first big hurdle in learning to read, and the kids have already jumped it without knowing it." And in 1977 Dr. Charles Shipman of HEW's special reading-improvement program said, "We've just finished a new study, and it shows a general increase in reading skills in the first three grades. I think commercials may have a lot to do with this. They're very cleverly designed to make a word register in your mind. A child sees the word on his screen while hearing it pronounced. Maybe the meaning is reinforced for him with cartoon drawings or a demonstration. Suddenly he's got it: the big connection between the meaning and the written and spoken word. He has the basic concept of reading."

Caleb Gattegno, innovative head of Educational Solutions, Inc. and author of *Towards a Visual Culture,* points out that kids use commercials to learn far more than reading. "Children's interest in commercials comes from another of the characteristics of growth. It is the only type of material that gives the child an opportunity to test whether his mind can exhaust the content of a complex situation. No other program is shown as often as are commercials, nor is any other so short and so focused on one aspect of life. Children view commercials with eagerness not because of their content (bras, cigars, trips, which for children are transcendental), but because they are opportunities to learn about one's self, one's memory, one's insights into the form of a message, the way material is used to obtain some ends, the order in which images follow each other, the words that are used and uttered."

And despite his contempt for the content of commercials, Gerald Lesser admits that most of *Sesame Street*'s best techniques derived from

KIDS SINGING: It's a lollypop with a (TOOT) on the top.

BOY: Peter Paul WhistlePop—(TOOT TOOT).

ANIMATED FACE: Another quality candy from Peter Paul. Indescribably delicious!

what their research found successful in commercials. The staff worked out certain behavioral objectives, what a child would do if the show succeeded, and, like ad writers aiming to get people to go to the store today, not tomorrow, they thought intensely about catching children's attention. "Commercial advertisements use animation and appealing music and sound effects, all designed to get the viewer's attention quickly and to hold it tightly for the commercial's short duration. . . . Equally obvious is music's function as an aid to memory in learning material in sequence." As Gattegno and others had suggested, their research turned up the fact that children pay more attention to whatever gets repeated most—usually commercials. In his book *Children and Television,* Lesser says,

Children seem to like certain pieces of televised material better after they have seen them several times. This seems especially true of short films or animation that build step by step to a humorous or incongruous outcome. This progression permits a child to anticipate each step in turn, saving the humorous outcome for the end but giving the child the safety of knowing that it indeed will occur after he has followed the episode through its earlier steps . . . Far from being merely a vehicle for simple, rote, or memorizable material (although it certainly accomplishes that purpose very well), the repeated segment can act as a mind-stretcher, permitting the child to return repeatedly to a subject completely explored during its first presentation. A child may experience even exact repetition of a segment differently each time, and thus explore its several facets.

Studying children's reactions to their first experiments, the *Sesame Street* researchers found that their own "J Commercial," an alphabet lesson using the commercial format, held the

PETER PAUL Children convince other children that they might like this combination of a toy and a lollypop; a cartoon adds a whistle and a joke to conclude the message.

children's interest almost completely. The only time their attention wandered from the J to the other characters was any time the J stood still, so the writers made the J jump around more. Not all commercials drive people crazy. In fact, they can even provide nontraditional education earlier, and in wider areas than some schools—or the programs they "sponsor."

Ironically, commercials may even train children to distrust the sponsors. Thomas Bever, who had worked with the famous child psychologist Piaget in Geneva, teamed up with the co-founder of an ad agency, Martin Smith, and his senior vice-president for market research, Thomas Johnson, plus Barbara Bengen, formerly director of the Children's Learning Center at Montefiore Hospital in New York, to find out just what children think about commercials. Borrowing Piaget's distinction between two ways of seeing the world, the figurative (we think what we see is true) and the operational (we test out our ideas in the real world and see if they really are true), the four researchers interviewed thirty-eight children ranging from four to twelve. They found that most five- and six-year-olds had trouble articulating the difference between fantasy and reality, and most could not distinguish between make-believe and lying, although they sensed there was a difference. Few kids at this age doubted adults, and almost none understood the economic reasons for commercials. Why are there commercials, then? the researchers asked the children. One five-year-old said, "It's to give actors time to rest." Given this naïveté, are these children vulnerable to ads? "Most of the young children we studied appeared to regard all television content as entertainment. They often confused programs with commercials and were unable to tell the difference between fantasy and reality in either." In sum, TV spots seem to have no more impact on most of them than the shows. But the children

can beg and nag for things, and parents will buy them.

As children reach the ages between seven and ten, though, inner conflict sets in. "According to our study, this group is the most vulnerable to the manipulation of TV advertisers." By seven, most can distinguish between reality and fantasy, and between innocent make-believe and lying. They see that folktales and fables are designed to teach lessons, but lies are not. Most understand that companies advertise for several reasons: "to sell products," "to get you to buy things." And by nine, children have been burned; they have asked for products, gotten them, and found them disappointing. "Chicken of the Sea is not the best tuna!" said one nine-year-old. And a ten-year-old girl said, "No More Tangles actually gave me knots!" Two girls exploded that "Long Nails didn't work." Most kids still have high hopes, though. "There is a chance that they might do the job, so we want to try them." Because they wavered between belief and disbelief, these children felt a fair amount of tension and anger at commercials, and they often suspected that something deceptive might be going on, though not sure exactly what. By the age of ten, many have solved the problem by deciding that commercials *always* lie. Understandably, the investigators and the *Harvard Business Review,* which printed their conclusions, felt quite troubled by this discovery.

By the time children are eleven or twelve, more balanced views win out, though. Children begin to understand the purpose of commercials the way adults do—so they can "put on more business. Then they can get more TV shows on the air, and they get more money for their product." Kids have now tested more claims and found that some are true, some are false. They can discriminate between an impression (what it *looks* like) and reality (what it actually tastes like or does). They also seem more willing to tolerate lying by adults, and television in general.

In conclusion, the authors of the study warn that "The 10-year-old's anger toward misleading advertising as well as the 11- and 12-year-old's increased tolerance of social hypocrisy raise serious questions about the role of TV advertising in the socialization of children." In other cultures only teenagers have to face the fact that the institutions of society lie to them. "But today TV advertising is stimulating pre-adolescent children to think about socially accepted hypocrisy. They may be too young to cope with such thoughts without permanently distorting their views of morality, society, and business." They question whether such exposure makes kids alert consumers; it may just make them cynical, and a bit callous. In fact, the editor of the *Harvard Business Review* worries, "What is most disconcerting to marketers and parents is that by age 11 when the two skill levels begin to coincide, most children have already become cynical—ready to believe that, like advertising, business and other institutions are riddled with hypocrisy."

So commercials may be teaching more than they intend about economic life in this country. Kids are not suckers, and after age ten many enjoy pointing out the exaggerations and possible lies in commercials. Scott Ward, a professor at the Harvard Business School, has found that eleven- and twelve-year-olds tend to turn away from commercials more often than seven-year-olds, define ads by the name of the sponsor, and remember more detail rather than random images.

Any company that sells to kids pays for similar research, but keeps its results secret, in order to beat competitors. Mattel Toys, for instance, takes its new commercials on a tour of Los Angeles movie theaters, advertising a 25-cent show with magicians, clowns, and prizes. The kids fill out questionnaires, picking the picture of the toy they like best (a new one by Mattel, next to three from competitors). David Chagall, a writer for *TV Guide,* described one such session: "First the kids see two minutes of commercials, then ten minutes of cartoons. Those are followed by another two minutes of commercials. Finally they are shown the main attraction, starring dolphins or other friendly beasts. When the program ends, a clown climbs onstage with some bad news. It seems the first questionnaires have been 'lost' by the magician or 'ruined' by another clown who spilled grape soda all over them. To qualify for the special drawing, the kids will have to fill out the questionnaire again. By comparing the results of the second set of commercials to the first, as well as to "control" commercials whose selling power is already known, Mattel researchers can determine which new commercials are the strongest child persuaders."

The results of most such research are kept locked in confidential files marked "Proprietary Information—Trade Secrets." As one consumer advocate, Robert Choate, said after he met these techniques when trying to market a game he had invented, "Industry doesn't want anyone to know about child research. Everything is secret, proprietary. Studies years old are locked away in sponsor and agency files—information that is used to make children into secret agents of big business in the home. . . . It's immoral because of the secrecy involved. They refuse to share their information with people who want to protect youngsters. We've got to find out what constitutes fair business communications aimed at children."

Mel Helitzer, who runs an ad agency devoted to the child market, told Chagall, "Children do benefit from research. They end up getting better products at cheaper prices and mass production is still the name of the game in America. A child's vulnerability means he or she comes to

TASTE TESTER: Doo–doo–doo. Hi, the Welchade Taste Tester here . . . with my newest friend.

Mommy or Daddy whining 'Buy me!' The real problem is the inability of many parents to say no. The second and ultimate weapon is for parents to turn off the TV set when it causes problems."

Helitzer published the results of his own research in the form of tips to the advertiser in a book called *The Youth Market.* His suggestions stay within the TV code but point out ways to get more children involved in pseudo-participation games, to prevent their utter disgust and disbelief, and to arouse their unconscious impulses. Helitzer found that children heard too much of Mom, so he recommends using a strong male voice to get their attention. "A limited use of children's voices saying, 'Great, wow, terrific,' can be highly effective. But these approving voices should be recorded off camera, so that they can be taken as those of other viewers rather than of participants in the commercial." Lots of slurpy sound effects help. If you show kids, make them real—sloppy, not too neat. Use boys more than girls: boys won't buy what girls recommend, but girls will long for what boys recommend. The older you get, use fancier visuals. Use animation; children believe in the Green

RED GRAPE: Howdy! I'm Welchade Red Grape Drink . . .

a great new kind of Welchade.

Giant, but not in pictures of real farmers ("They're just actors.") Any participation hooks the viewer, so show how the product can be turned into a game. "Heltizer Advertising helped the Arlington Hat Company sell over 750,000 spinner top hats by showing 37 uses for the product in a quick-cut 60-second commercial." Invent tongue-twisters, so kids try to say them. Tell jokes. "Hey, you want a Hawaiian punch? . . . *whop!*" Keep the package on screen, and use the name a lot. Put Mom in the picture to suggest she approves and to make Mom think she will win the child's love by buying the product. Put in plenty of magic; use before-and-after segments; make up new words and goofy situations. "Advertising to kids should be fun," says Heltizer. "Let's keep it that way!"

Historically, however, commercials for kids have not been a lark. Sixteen minutes an hour used to be devoted to commercials, and many were made by the host of the show, so children had a rough time recognizing just when a commercial had begun; this made it harder even for eleven-year-olds to tune them out. During 1955 Dr. Frances Horwich, "Principal" of *Ding Dong School,* habitually chatted to children about the

WELCH'S Children pay attention to cartoons, so Welch's used one to introduce a new product in their Welchade line.

pretty red pills she had in her hand, and how easy they were to take. Next time the kids went to the drug store with Mom, she said, they should nag her to get the right brand. These vitamin pill ads provoked *The New York Times* critic, Jack Gould, to complain, "To put it as mildly as possible, Dr. Horwich has gone a step too far in letting a commercial consideration jeopardize her responsibility to the young children whose faith and trust she solicits.... Using a child's credibility to club a parent into buying something is reprehensible under the best of circumstances. But in the case of a product bearing on a child's health, it is inexcusable." Letters to the editor agreed, en masse, but nothing changed. Herb Sheldon, a kiddy-show star of the day, boasted to *Ad Age,* "Children are living, talking records of what we tell them every day." And many sponsors went beyond buying the host's spurious authority, applying motivational research and extravagant production techniques to spots designed for children. Toy commercials used fancy lenses, tricky angles, and slow-motion/high-speed effects to make model cars seem to race through the living room; announcers said that dolls could walk "just like you" when in fact you had to hold them up and push them forward; spotlights made every game seem spec-

tacular; announcers kept telling kids to get Mom to buy it for them; prices were rarely mentioned; you never knew if batteries were included; and superlatives dropped like the best gumdrops from the most fabulous sky.

In 1961 the National Association of Broadcasters finally issued some guidelines for toy ads: no more superlatives or "bests," no more animation, since children tended to imagine the product as being as clever as it was in the cartoon; in sum, no more glamour. Now a sponsor had to mention it if a toy needed assembling or extra batteries. As a result, toy commercials have become some of the most honest spots on TV. And in 1970 the NAB issued a five-point bulletin, telling kidvid advertisers that they should limit any fantasy elements to the first third of the spot, and no kids or toys could show up in these scenes; no one could endorse the product; no comparisons would be made to competitors; the last five seconds would show the product the way you find it in the store; no camera or sound techniques could be used that distorted size, value, or performance. Of course, some toymakers simply pulled their spots out of kiddy shows and put them on the early prime time hours, when fantasy can fill the whole spot and no one has to waste five seconds showing the

KID: Here come the Super Shot Racers.

ANNOUNCER: They accelerate . . . and keep on going . . . up to 65 feet. And crash after crash, they keep on running.

FATHER: Hi, Son. Hey! What's that? Helen! . . . Helen! What's with this blue stuff?

MOTHER: Oh, it's a new toothpaste—AIM. I just got it.

FATHER: Have you flipped? What about fluoride? And you know what the dentist said. The kid's cavity-prone.

MOTHER: Henry, AIM has stannous fluoride just like our old toothpaste.

FATHER: OK, so it has fluoride. So, what's wrong with the fluoride we've been using?

MARX A realistic scene, with dirt, and bumps—no super graphics, no wild camera angles—the result of new rules on toy commercials. (*opposite*)

LEVER BROTHERS Aim family drama: Mother and Father worry about Son's teeth, but he brushes with Aim, reaching for the back teeth. Father does not want to give up the old toothpaste, but he has been outmaneuvered by the important members of the family. (*above*)

MOTHER: Look, Henry, AIM is less abrasive than the leading fluoride paste.

SON: I like it! It tastes good!

product just sitting there at the end. Two million dollars in toy ads dropped out of TV altogether during 1971, and, since the hosts could no longer charm kids into buying the products, sponsors nixed the shows, and many local ones closed.

The gloves were off now. In 1971 the newly formed Action for Children's Television—a group of concerned parents—went to the FCC and asked that TV stations be required to produce fourteen hours a week of daily programming for kids, all without commercials. One hundred thousand signatures on petitions and letters backed up ACT, the advertisers and broadcasters tried to combat such a frightening idea, and the FCC finally accepted a measure of self-regulation by the advertisers and refused to ban commercials from kiddy shows on the grounds that the shows would probably go off the air if they did not take advertising revenues. In return, on January 1, 1976, the NAB finally reduced the time allotted to commercials to 9½ minutes per hour of programming on weekends, and to 12 minutes an hour during the week. (The code only allows 9½ minutes per hour during adult prime time.)

Producing children's commercials has become a lot more complicated because of these new critics and censors, and writing the spots has become an intricate hell, "subject to as much discipline and scrutiny as a State Department public statement," as adman Don Goldberg warned readers of *Writer's Digest*. He complains that *Sesame Street* can do everything he may not, just because they are supposedly educational. "It just seems to me that those award-winning kids' shows—the ones that are recommended by the National Education Association—have been able to use all the techniques they can afford under the name of 'entertainment.' And if TV can exist as a separate reality for kids, then maybe TV commercials should be allowed to exist, too, as imagination decides, within the realm of that separate reality." Goldberg's point may be self-serving, but it has some strength. If parents are really worried about children's understanding of reality—rather than just their embarrassing and unhealthy purchases—then they should censor the shows the same way they do the commercials. But, in fact, liberal middle-class parents like children to be "sold" on some ideas; and *Sesame Street* uses the techniques of commercials to propagandize for middle-class ideas of "the way things should be": the main adult males are businessmen; their word is always accepted without doubt or question; children are shown adapting to but not changing the situation invented for them by the grown-up men; memorization of language is more important than learning that reading is an extension of listening and speaking. As The Network Project notes in *Down Sesame Street:*

Beyond the rudimentary skills of reading and arithmetic, children reared by Children's Television Workshop productions are trained to respect the differences of others, cooperate with all members of society, love humanity—in short, to become exactly what social institutions expect of them.

Nor are these lessons presented incidentally; as a following appendix (B) documents, they are carefully engineered by the Workshop's collection of psychologists, assisted by others from government agencies and academic institutions. Their efforts assure that CTW productions broaden the child by molding his social personality. Despite the pretentious aims of CTW, it is educating children not for their own sake, but for their value to society.

Since the protest movement rises from the middle class, it does not challenge the right of corporations to produce dangerous food and toys and to advertise them; the concerned parents simply try to remove the more embarrassingly *obvious* forms of exploitation from the air.

And some of these products really are dangerous. The continuous din of cereal and junk food

SINGERS: You get ten friends in every bar.
Caramello.

Ten friends in every bar.

Ten friends in every bar.

CADBURY The elemental pitch to children: with this candy bar, you will make friends. Like flies.

ads has aroused the disgust of FTC Chairman Pertschuk, as well as that of consumer advocate Robert Choate, who calls an average hour of kiddy shows "refrigerator roulette," and says that "A child is invited ten times per hour to establish food habits which his dentist or doctor will later deplore." People are moving around less than they did in the 1930's; and they are eating more calories; a late-Sixties University of Georgia study showed that the cardboard cereal boxes themselves, if eaten with milk and raisins, gave as much nutrition as any but the most sophisticated cereals then on the market, such as Life or Special K. ACT has petitioned for a ban or at least restrictions on advertising of highly sugared foods to children, and the FTC has announced it will consider it—thus setting off a flurry of charges, countercharges, with cerealmakers blaming candymakers for children's eating habits, and vice versa.

The FTC never hurries its hearings, though. So the advertisers and the broadcasters may work out some neat self-regulation before the government can make up its mind what rules banning ads for sugary foods would not violate the First Amendment right to free speech. Is it a deceptive practice to encourage people to eat something that if overeaten could give them cavities? Will outlawing such advertising do any good? Stay tuned into the mid-Eighties. In Canada, when the government banned all ads on children's programs, the sponsors just shifted into the family shows in the evening. Corrective advertising doesn't seem to be particularly effective, either: a psychologist at the University of Toronto, Kenneth O'Bryan, who has helped apply ad techniques to *Sesame Street,* said that the thirty-second spot is the best educational tool he has seen on TV, except when it advertised good health. Children, it seems, ignore public service messages such as those created in the U.S. by ACT plugging apples and oranges instead of candy.

Thanks to the pressures brought by the reformists, commercials aimed at children may keep *looking* less offensive, while still sneaking their tempting message past the regulators. And of course, now the commercials for children are even better than many of the shows they interrupt because they *look* more realistic, more informative, than ever before. Imagine trying to eliminate "illusions" from the surrounding shows the way the regulators have done with spots.

Regular programming is not expected to tell the truth, evidently. In fact, it is allowed to appeal to the same unconscious impulses played on by so many commercials for grown-ups. So the shows themselves go on violating all these rules. The hero leaps into the air (unrealistic portrayal of movement), blasts out a magic signal (exaggerated sound effects), which casts a spell over the villains (fantasy powers), then descends to massive applause (no heroic shots). Or the horn on the car lights up and flashes (obtrusive video devices of a psychedelic nature), warning the hero that the villains are coming. In one sequence the heroine touches her necklace, says a few words, and—through the miracle of fast cuts—becomes the goddess Isis. ("Pop-ons and wipes are unacceptable.") Plants get up and walk around in cartoons. ("It should be positively disclosed that toys which require manual manipulation do not 'walk' or 'dance' on their own. You *make* them walk.") Good and bad guys in cartoons and realistic shows slam through walls, bounce onto the roads, shoot each other, fight, stab, gnaw, and claw. ("Violence for its own sake and the detailed dwelling upon brutality or physical agony, by sight or by sound, are not permissible.") Gadgets freeze people by rays, transport people by beams, preserve people from boiling oil with mysterious robots. ("The presentation must not, by copy or demonstration, involve a material deception as to the characteristics, performance, or appearance of the product.") At the moment, then, even spots promoting gooky cereals and sticky goober bars have more apparent reality per second than *Mr. Magoo.*

If people wanted reality, they'd turn off TV. We love unreality, though, and only worry when we notice that children do, too. Why do parents, who buy tires, wines, film, cards, transmissions, cars they first saw on TV, get upset when children ask for something *they* saw on TV? Maybe it's like a bad habit. Kids doing it reminds us that *we* do.

Cleaning up children's commercials only glosses over the surface: it leaves the basic fictions untouched. So children's commercials are like slightly daring movies: they are not exactly rated X, but they are not good clean wholesome G banality, either. Perhaps every commercial break should begin with a card saying: Parental Guidance Recommended.

and still the best!

at first glance many of the commercials in this book seem uniquely American, the product of a certain time and place. But looked at more deeply, our commercials reveal a very human yearning for experiences so universal, so common, that even without words many American spots can be understood around the world. In this sense, commercials may be the myths of our electronic culture.

Thus, particularly when we are attuned to our own period and its concerns, we may only be aware of the superficial meanings of a commercial (it is about a Japanese car, the car can stand up under pressure), whereas our unconscious may be reveling in the less obvious implications (I can smash it, I can wrap it around toll booths). And we may respond to a commercial in an analytic fashion, either as someone who creates them, or as someone who criticizes them, or in a subjective fashion, simply absorbing them, using them for our own conscious and unconscious purposes. Usually our response mixes both styles of reaction: we try to unmask the commercial's real intention, while at the same time we may get sucked into the story and feel it as if it were a real experience. Hence our mixed feelings about most commercials, and our conviction that we really don't believe them.

Commercials show us the whole mythology of upper-middle-class existence but they don't help us pay for it. If we are poor, we may "buy" that way of thinking without being able to buy the products. As Ronald Barthes says of French advertising in *Mythologies*, "The bourgeoisie is constantly absorbing into its ideology a whole section of humanity which does not have its basic status and cannot live up to it except in imagination, that is, at the cost of an immobilization and an impoverishment of consciousness . . . it is as if from the moment when a typist earns

DANNON YOGURT Most fondly remembered commercial.

(MEN SINGING)

and we're not saying Dannon Yogurt will help you live longer.

By the way, Temur Vanacha thought Dannon was really fine yogurt.

ANNOUNCER: In Soviet Georgia, where they eat a lot of yogurt,

a lot of people live past 100. Of course, many things affect longevity,

But Dannon is a wholesome, natural food that has active cultures.

Many other yogurts don't.

He ought to know.

He's been eating yogurt for 105 years.

BENNY GOODMAN: Do you know me?

REBECCA ANN KING: Do you know me?

WILLIAM MILLER: I ran for Vice-President of the United States in '64.

SAM ERVIN: I'm just a plain ol' country lawyer.

MEL BLANC: Despicable!

BOB FOSSE: But still people don't know my face.

BILL BLASS: Do you know me?

JIM HENSEN: I created the Muppets.
MUPPETS: Big deal!

NORMAN FELL: So because I travel, I got the
American Express Card. *(Continued)*

sixty dollars a week she recognizes herself in the big wedding of the bourgeoisie." The myth helps her imagine she is rich, even at *le Wimpy*.

Whether aimed at lower classes, or children growing up, commercials sometimes function the way anthropologist Joseph Campbell describes myths operating in primitive cultures:

The aim of education in the primitive, archaic, and Oriental spheres has always been and will no doubt continue to be, for many centuries, not primarily to enlighten the mind concerning the nature of the universe, but to create communities of shared experience for the engagement of the sentiments of the growing individual in the matters of chief concern to the local group. The unsocialized thought and feeling of the very young child are egocentric but not socially dangerous. When the primary urges of the adolescent remain unsocialized, however, they become inevitably a threat to the harmony of the group. The paramount function of all myth and ritual, therefore, has always been, and surely must continue to be, to engage the individual, both emotionally and intellectually, in the local organization. And this aim is best effected—as we have seen—through a solemn conjuring up of intensely shared experiences by virtue of which the whole system of childhood fantasy and spontaneous belief is engaged and fused with the functioning system of the community.

Myths generally justify and motivate some ritual act. And each commercial invites us to participate in at least one ritual: purchase. Through purchase, we are told, we will experience maximum orgasm, see a psychedelic light show, gain the power to wreck whole fleets of trucks at one blow, and clean our filthy home in two seconds.

Commercials, like myths, teach children the important illusions of a culture; they are one way we train our children to read, count, compare (bad versus good, better, best, and jumbo), follow stories, sing along, memorize, and doubt

AMEX Biggest tease: who are all those people, anyway?

claims. In brief, commercials give children the superficial markings of our nation, the tags of our tribe, the secret handshakes that show we are all middle-class Americans. But underneath this local training, children eventually learn, like their parents, to expect that a gadget will cure them, cheer them up, calm them down, and clean house like magic. And commercials raise children to "participate" in this adult ritual, the economy, by sending in premiums, getting Mom to buy something for them, by quoting from commercials at school. Thus the simplest ritual, that of following along when a commercial comes on, gradually prepares our children for the more complicated lifelong routines that our society demands.

Myths also help us express, and control in a safe way, impulses that could potentially tear our society apart. In primitive cultures, people actually got drunk and made love in night-and-day orgies, and sacrificed human beings, but these activities were carefully limited to a certain phase of the lunar year, and no other. The myths justified this physical expression of the impulses toward sex, craziness, and violence, while also isolating such activity from ordinary life; in a way, hearing the myth at another time served as a substitute for the rites. We are no longer primitive, but our commercials do show numberless visions of the goddess of love unveiling herself, asking us to undress, take it off, let her stroke us, come fly with her, wear nothing at all. She tells us, "I don't wear panties any more." She urges us, "Do it, come 'doo it." But, of course, there is a screen in the way. And commercials let us imagine blowing up—and reassembling—a camera or a car, tossing cars from planes, from buildings, from waterfalls, smashing watches or shooting locks. Our natural and childish impulses get made into larger-than-life scenes, isolated from real experience by the fact that they are on TV. And the way to reexperience these sensations, at least in our unconscious,

BENNY GOODMAN: Restaurants and night clubs.

CHARLES CONRAD: Why, someday I may even use it on the moon.

ANNOUNCER: To apply for an American Express Card, call 800-528-8000,

GEORGE GALLUP: I use it for business traveling and entertaining.

WILLIAM MILLER: In Tokyo, Paris, and upstate New York.

SAM ERVIN: With this, maybe they'll treat me like somebody important.

JACK GILFORD: Even if they don't know this adorable face.

or look for this display wherever the Card is welcomed.

BARBARA FELDON: The American Express Card.

ANNOUNCER: This is the story of two crops.

Carrots. And Weyerhaeuser trees.

Plenty of sun.

Some rain. And lots of care.

And Weyerhaeuser thins the forest, too, to let in the sun.

The small logs go to make pulp and plywood. However, there is one big difference.

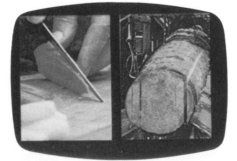

Forty-five years after planting seedlings, you have mature trees. For lumber, paper, and plywood.

It'd be a lot simpler if we could grow trees as fast as carrots. But nature doesn't really work that way.

Both take fertile soil.

You thin the carrots so there's more room
to grow bigger carrots.

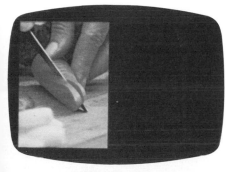

Forty-five days after you plant carrots—
you have carrots to eat.

Weyerhaeuser. The tree growing
company.

is to sacrifice another coin in that basic ritual
of America, the buy.

But underneath such locally useful integra-
tion of our raucous impulses into society, myths
serve a deeper function. They open up awe in
us. They remind us of miracles and of wild instincts within ourselves. Primitive myths encouraged ecstatic states, direct communication with
the divine, and careful performance of the rituals handed down to people from the god or
goddess. Homer's myths made spirits walk the
land; in Britain the Druids' tales showed ghosts
and witches worked with elves and fairies to
protect the wise; but our myths are commercial.
The directors and actors, the producers and
writers of our commercials may resemble the
participants in these primitive rituals in that
they often try to believe, want to believe, in the
reality of what they do, and, failing that, they
make sure *we* believe. And what do commercials encourage us to believe?

This mythic world is magic. Voices in the
air, not attached to bodies, regularly order us
around in commercials, take care of us, and give
us advice, just like spirits. In this realm we can
change the shape of people who have indigestion, make a package of gum as big as a tree, or
slice apart a car in an instant. We can fly over
golf courses, over the planet, over galaxies; we
can drive on water. By mysterious devices, we
can make the blind see. We can tame a wild
bear to follow us into a bar; we can make a
wild deer eat Oreos and go where we want; we
can teach koala bears, cats, and elephants to talk,
sing, and dance. Commercials resemble the
dreams of a primitive hunter or child in their
faith in magic.

One central figure dominates many myths—
the great Mother, who transforms herself into a

WEYERHAEUSER Most ecological pitch for a company that cuts trees.

SINGERS: Baseball, hot dogs, apple pie . . .

thousand forms; sometimes she appears as Mother Nature, sometimes as Mother Earth, sometimes as Lady Fortune, other times as Aphrodite. And in our commercials we see the great Mom go through a hundred transformations in a day, always reappearing with a bottle, a glow, or a rhymed spell to chase the troubles of the suffering representative of humanity. She is the horrid fat harridan checking for dirt in the bathroom, the feathery grandma clutching memories of love, the sprightly WASP woman of fifty abandoning the ancestral home, the chubby fierce huntress forcing a young boy to eat white paste, the stupid but affectionate nurse smothering her child in too many medicinal syrups, Mother Nature making Grand Canyon quake, or a hundred-and-twenty-year-old Soviet yenta eating yogurt. She survives the death of Dad, innumerable times. She makes and pampers the universal baby. And, when the mood strikes, she reaches for another potion, and turns from a gray-haired Mom into a thirtyish swinger who can cut through greasy dirt with another supernatural brew.

and Chevrolet.

Thus, in many ways commercials act as contemporary myths. They awe us, surprising us with trompe l'oeil miracles. They arouse our deepest impulses toward sex, violence, and faith, and they express these instincts while at the same time keeping that expression aesthetic, rather than physical, thus saving our society from the potential chaos of orgies and massacre. Instead of the real thing, we are encouraged to perform a substitute act, a symbolic gesture, in which we put coins on a counter and pick up a magic potion or a symbolic object. And after this ritual we are expected to experience the pleasures hypnotically suggested before: an imaginary ecstasy.

ANNOUNCER: In case you're wondering . . .

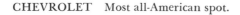

CHEVROLET   Most all-American spot.

SINGERS: Baseball . . .

and Chevrolet.

Baseball, hot dogs . . . .

and apple pie . . .

(MUSIC)

They go together, in the good old

USA.

this message is brought to you . . .

by baseball, hot dogs, apple pie . . .

and America's favorite car.

hot dogs . . .

apple pie, and Chevrolet.

GONDOLIER: Of love I sing . . .

la-la-la-la.

WIFE: My powder didn't work.

ANNOUNCER: Those dirty rings . . . You tried scrubbing, even spraying, and still . . .

Try Wisk.

Wisk sinks in and starts to clean

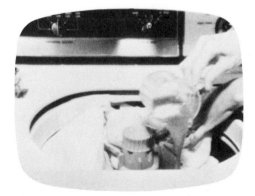

Then gets your whole wash really clean.

HUSBAND: No more ring-around-the-collar-la-la!

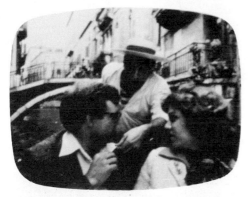

But you've got ring-around-the-collar-la-la.

you've got ring-around-the-collar.

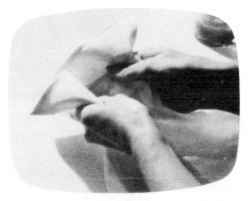

before you start to wash.

ANNOUNCER: Use Wisk around the collar for ring-around-the-collar.

Most programs on TV seem oddly old-fashioned. They imitate films; they take too long; they show people, not just cars, getting hurt; they let lovers get into bed together, rather than just talk about it and kiss; they spend less on convincing and exotic sets; they hardly polish their scenes to the split-second to persuade us and disturb us. They do not demand any ritual follow-up afterward. They lack the glamour, the panache, of commercials.

Commercials work faster, do more magic in less time, arouse more emotions, provoke more real actions in the daily world, keep the economy dizzily spinning. Commercials are not radio news with slides; they are not nineteenth-century novels done up in heavy costumes; they are not even nineteen-forties films redone in color for unsuspecting audiences. In an hour of TV we are likely to see all these aftertraces from several generations of myths—the primitive, the print, the modern film, and the post-modern scene, all jumbled up. Commercials move in fast; tightly edited, quickly paced, their style fits TV better; their contents express contemporary conflicts better, being at once more "primitive" and more highly technological than the programs. If, as Americans believe, the new is better than the old, and the hard sell beats the soft, then commercials today are the best myth on TV.

This chapter is a collection of favorite spots, a treasury of our most expensive mythology.

WISK Most irritating.

BOY: Hey! Someone tell Grandma.

The movers are here. Grandma.
Grandma.

WARREN: Grandma, how come you
have to move from your house?
OLD LADY: Because it's too big.

OLD LADY: Well, I certainly hope so.

Oh look!
WARREN: What's in there?

OLD LADY: This is very special.
These are my cards.

You remember this one. It's the
one you sent me last
spring . . . when I was in the
hospital.

WARREN: Yeah, I picked it out
myself.

OLD LADY: Made me feel better.

I don't need all this room now that everybody's got their own home.

WARREN: Can I come and visit you at your new apartment?

These are birthday cards, and get well cards. . . .

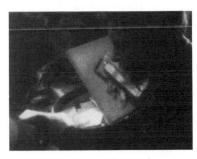

and all the lovely cards people have sent me since I was as young as you are.

WARREN: Who's this one from?
OLD LADY: So long ago.

WARREN: Who's it from?
OLD LADY: Your Granddad sent . . . *(Continued)*

HALLMARK Most nostalgic moving day.

that to me on our first anniversary.
WARREN: What's an anniversary?

OLD LADY: Well, it's kinda like a
birthday. Only it's for the number of
years two people have been
married.

(MUSIC)

(MUSIC)

OLD LADY: (GIVES AN UPLIFTING SIGH)

PATTY: Grandma.
BETTY: Come on, you two.

PATTY: Look what I found!
OLD LADY: Oh! I love that hat.

BETTY: Mother. The movers are here. Come on, we have to get going. Do you have everything you want from up . . . here?

OLD LADY: The movers can pack the rest.
BETTY: Mama?

You don't want to forget this one. Your birthday.

(MUSIC)

Look at Michael.

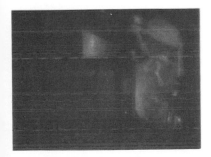

ANNOUNCER: Greeting cards.

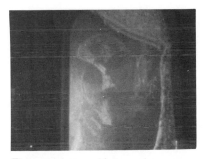

They can keep a lifetime of memories safe and secure.

Hallmark. When you care enough to send the very best.

Prepared by Doyle Dane Bernbach for American Tourister Luggage

ITT   Most earth-shattering. With ITT optical fibers, you won't need to hire a giant to rip out skyscrapers to replace the pipes below. (*opposite*)
AMERICAN TOURISTER   Best suitcase for gorillas. (*above*)

(MUSIC COMES UP)

ANNOUNCER: You may be the last to know you have a foot odor problem.

(MUSIC UP) . . .

(MUSIC UNDER)

ANNOUNCER: Foot odor happens.

Sprays on dry . . . helps keep feet dry and odor-free.

(MUSIC UP)

It works.

SCHOLL   A knockout. (*above*)
PARKAY   Most talkative tub of margarine. (*below right*)

(MUSIC CONTINUES)

Play it safe with Scholl Dry
Anti-Perspirant

(COMPUTER SOUNDS) ANNOUNCER: At Emery,

we can tell you where your package is in just ten seconds.

In fact, thanks to a computer tracking system,

that works like radar, we can tell you when it was picked up,

when it took off, what flight it's on, when it lands,

when it's delivered, and how it's delivered.

So we keep an eye on your package until it's right under your nose.

The Emery computer tracking system.

It's the only thing in air freight that can keep up with Emery.

EMERY   Television watching itself. (*above*)

ALKA-SELTZER   The phrase became a national whine, an instant joke. (*opposite*)

(RESTAURANT NOISES) MAN: Came to this little place.

Waiter says, "Try this, you'll like it."

"What's this?" "Try it, you'll like it."

"But what is it?"

"Try it, you'll like it."

So I tried it.

Thought I was gonna die.

Took two Alka-Seltzer.

(PLOP, PLOP . . . FIZZ)

ANNOUNCER: Alka-Seltzer neutralizes all the acid your stomach has churned out.

For your upset stomach and headache, take Alka-Seltzer, and feel better fast.

MAN: Alka-Seltzer works. "Try it, you'll like it."

MEL BROOKS' VOICE: Don't write with a peach. If you write with a peach, you'll get a very wet letter.

Never . . . repeat . . . never try to write with a prune. Your words will come out wrinkled and dopey.

Let's face it. The only fruit you can write with is a Bic Banana. Because the Bic Banana is a fine-line marker. Not to be confused with a ballpoint.

You're writing a letter to your son, right? Right. Usually you write, "Dear Son, how are you? I'm fine. . . ."

You write that same letter with a Bic Banana and you get: "Dear Sonny, I miss your face. Mom." See what a nice letter it writes?

And it comes in colors. Most fruits only come in one color. Except grapes. Which come in two colors. And, of course, pits and pitless.

Look, if you must write with a fruit, write with a Bic Banana.

Only 29¢. Your best buy in writing fruit.

BIC BANANA   Best advice. (*above*)
ARM & HAMMER   Best cartoon reminder to clean your refrigerator. (*opposite*)

(MUFFLED SOUNDS OF ARGUING): Help, help! Keep your smelly hands off me!

OLD BOX: Remember me? I'm the box of baking soda you left in the refrigerator. Back then I could really absorb those food odors. . . .

ONION: Onion Power!

OLD BOX: Ah, if a new box doesn't show up soon, a lot of food's gonna get spoiled. . . . Aah!

BAD FOODS: Oh oh!

GOOD FOODS: We're saved!

NEW BOX: You foods are gonna keep your smells to yourselves!

BAD FOODS: Party pooper!

ANNOUNCER: If you can't remember the last time you changed the baking soda . . .

it's probably time to change it again.

NEW BOX: Any last words?

OLD BOX: What took you so long?

On December 5, 1973, at a rifle range outside Los Angeles,

a high-powered 30 caliber rifle . . .

was fired at a distance of 40 yards

Repeat: did not open.

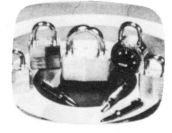

Whatever your protection needs, there's a Master Lock ready to do the job.

MASTER LOCK   Best aim. (*above*)

STOUFFER'S   When the gang comes to dinner, and likes it, this lasagna wins the prize: most relief. (*near right*)

HARTFORD INSURANCE GROUP   Most grown-up animal star. (*far right*)

to try and open this Master padlock.

The Master Lock Model No. 15 sustained considerable damage. . . .

but did not open.

ANNOUNCER: The best protection is prevention.

(MUSIC STARTS) . . .

The next time you're in an Italian neighborhood, go into a grocery store

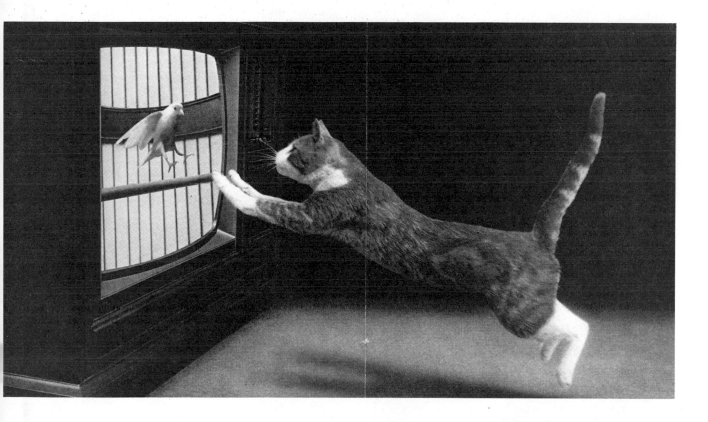

RONZONI Most ethnic pitch. (*opposite*)
GTE SYLVANIA Best practical joke. (*above*)

and ask for spaghetti. No particular brand.

See what brand you get.

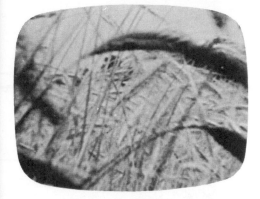

ANNOUNCER: You get more fun out of gardening with good tools . . .

designed for the job you have to do.

We carry a wide variety of fine Ames tools.

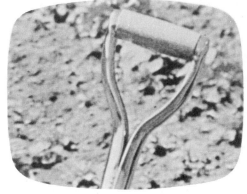

They're polished . . . sharpened . . . welded . . . forged . . .

serrated . . . chromed . . . coated and cushioned.

To get the job done quickly . . . easily . . . cleanly.

Ames . . . lawn and garden tools . . . they've helped

America grow since 1774.

AMES   Most beautiful shovels. (*above*)

I like my men in English Leather, or nothing at all.

It's a miracle!

ENGLISH LEATHER Sexiest pool hustle. (*above*)
XEROX Most miraculous. (*right*)

ANNOUNCER: Have you ever wondered what the man who drives the snowplow drives to get to work?

Prepared by Doyle Dane Bernbach for Volkswagen of America, Inc.

VOLKSWAGEN   Beyond words.